دراسات إسلامية

ISLAMIC STUDIES

BOOK: I   للصف الأول المتوسط

INTERMEDIATE LEVEL (GRADE SEVEN)

by

Abu Ameenah Bilal Philips

ISBN 1 898649 50 2

British Library Cataloguing in Publication Data.
A catalogue record for this book is available from the British Library.

Published by: Al-Hidaayah Publishing and Distribution

Distributed by: Al-Hidaayah Publishing and Distribution
P.O. Box 3332
Birmingham
B10 0UH
United Kingdom

Tel: 0121 753 1889
Fax: 0121 753 2422
Email: mail@al-hidaayah.co.uk
Website: www.al-hidaayah.co.uk

CONTENTS

FOREWORD

At its inception more than a decade ago, the English Section of Manarat Al-Riyadh Schools was faced with the acute problem of looking for an Islamic Education textbook — or a series of textbooks — that introduced Islaam in an easy, comprehensible manner to Muslim school children. Though there were a few Islamic books available on the market then, none of them suitably met the needs of school-going children, especially from the point of view of the standard we had set for our students.

We approached Mr. Bilal Philips, a Canadian native speaker of English, and a graduate of the Islamic University of Madeenah, to assist us in developing an Islamic Education syllabus catering to the educational and spiritual needs of the Manarat pupils. Mr. Philips was then doing a masters in Islamic Theology at King Saud University, but despite his academic engagements he very kindly agreed to undertake this propitious task. He also extended his services to teach that syllabus to students of various age groups at the English Section of Manarat Al-Riyadh Schools.

It was during this period that he prepared extensive notes which formed the basis for this book and the other textbooks that are to follow, Inshaallah, in the near future. During the ten years in which these notes were taught, they were continually revised in the light of feedback from students and suggestions/advice received from colleagues and parents.

Several years of painstaking efforts to improve the quality and content of these notes and the laborious task of simplifying the language and expression to a level appropriate to the pupils' understanding of Islaam have now culminated in the publication of this fore-runner of a series of Islamic Education textbooks. These texts will be suitable not only as a textbook but also as a general guide to further the average person's understanding of Islaam.

Abu Ameenah Bilal Philips is a qualified teacher of Islamic Education and a research scholar who has published an impressive array of books on various aspects of Islaam. Presently, he is working on his doctoral dissertation at the University of Wales, U.K.

We at Manarat Al-Riyadh International Islamic School believe that this project will bridge the gap that has hitherto existed in the availability of Islamic Education textbooks in the English language for children studying at English medium schools. We sincerely hope that this book, apart from meeting the requirements of curriculum planners, will be a great success among pupils.

The teaching staff and the entire student body of Manarat Al-Riyadh International Islamic School pray to Allah to reward Mr. Bilal Philips for his service to Islaam in writing these books.

Rizk Ibrahim Kamh
Principal
English Section
Manarat Al Riyadh International School
Riyadh, Saudi Arabia

21st November, 1990.

PREFACE

This text is based on the Islamic Studies syllabus covering the following four major areas of study: *Tawheed, Tafseer, Hadeeth* and *Fiqh*. It is therefore assumed that the "Qur'anic skills" of reading and recitation would be covered in Arabic classes, and "Islamic History" including the *Seerah* (Biography of the Prophet [ﷺ]) would be included either in the Social Studies syllabus as a major topic, or taught as a separate subject.

Aims of the Course

1. To acquaint the student with the uniqueness of the Islamic concept of God and how it affects man's relationship with God, with his fellow man and with the creation in which he lives. This may be achieved through the study of *Tawheed*. (Islamic Monotheism).

2. To introduce the student to the meanings of the final book of revelation, the Qur'aan, and their revelance to daily life, as opposed to the ritual recitation of the Qur'anic text without any realization of its meanings whatsoever. This could be developed during the study of the *Tafseers* (commentaries) of the *Soorahs* (Qur'anic chapters).

3. To familiarize the student with his Islamic rights and obligations and present a clear and authentic picture of how they may be fulfilled. This would best be accomplished in the detailed study of *Fiqh* (Islamic law) and *Tawheed*.

4. To develop in the student a realization that Islaam is built on firm, clear, logical principles and that it is not merely a collection of irrelevant cultural practices handed down from earlier generations. This can be done through the study of the sciences *(Usool)* of *Hadeeth* (Prophetic traditions), *Fiqh* and *Tafseer*.

5. To identify and build an Islamic character in the student through the study of Islamic Ethics which is, no doubt, an essen-

tial component of any Islamic Education curriculum. This field of study is to be found in the Prophetic traditions *(Hadeeth)* which have been carefully chosen for in-depth study and discussion at all levels.

Method of Presentation

The order in which the topics have been arranged is based on the aims and their priority. *Tawheed* represents the most fundamental principle of Islaam, while the teachings of Islaam are based on the Qur'aan (the understanding of which is called *Tafseer)*, and the *Sunnah* (the teachings of the Prophet (ﷺ) contained in *Hadeeths)*. The application of the teachings falls within the frame work of *Fiqh* (Islamic Law). The teacher, however, is free to vary the order according to the class response and his or her personal preferences, as long as the whole syllabus is covered.

Arabic terminology should be used and properly pronounced wherever possible, and students should be held responsible for understanding the important transliterated forms mentioned in the text. Terms written in Arabic script should not be emphasized unless the whole class is able to read and write in Arabic script. Accordingly, the teacher's treatment of Arabic terms should take into account the fact that in any given grade, there may be students who are raw beginners in Arabic. In this way, the teacher may avoid double penalization of a student whereby a poor mark in Arabic automatically results in a poor mark in Islamic Education.

Discussion about each of the topics of the syllabus should be encouraged among the students and reasoned explanations should be given to their questions where possible. Ample time should also be allotted at the end of each class for general questions, as Islamic Education covers all aspects of human life and the Islamic Studies teacher will also be required to fulfil the role of counsellor or student advisor. The Islamic Studies teacher should attempt to find answers to all the students' questions by making personal research using advanced reference material and by cont acting outstanding Islamic scholars in their region. The student may also be given either individual or group term research projects on the topics, to further stimulate discussion and interest.

At the end of this book there is a selected bibliography of available English reference works used in the preparation of this text, as well as works which may be used by both teachers and students to obtain further information on the topics covered.

Division of Lessons

The material covered by the four major topics represents a full school year's work; therefore the sub-topics have been distributed over two semesters according to a timetable allotting two to three lessons per week for Islamic studies. Consequently, three weeks have been given to each topic for study, review and testing. Questions are given at the end of each sub-topic as homework, which should be reviewed before beginning the next sub-topic. A general review of the material of the sub-topics may be given at the end of the third week followed by a test. If time constraints develop, wherein it becomes necessary to omit a part of the syllabus, it is advisable to aim at exposure to all of the major topics and confine syllabus reduction to the number of *Hadeeths* and/or *Soorahs* (chapters of the Qur'aan covered in *Tafseer*) prescribed for detailed study. The following is a sample work scheme which has been used at Manaret Al-Riyadh Schools, with some variations, for nearly ten years.

Sample Work Scheme

Grade: 7 First Term

TOPIC	SUB-TOPIC	WEEK
TAWHEED	Categories of Tawheed	1
	'Ebaadah (The Purpose of Creation)	2
	Review and Test	3

Grade: 7 Second Term

Content

A concerted effort has been made to insure that all of the material contained in this series of texts is authentic. This is of utmost importance where the dissemination of Islamic knowledge is concerned. It has been the practice in books of this type, especially those prepared for children, to take great liberties in presentation. However, this should not be the case, because it is from such simple incorrect beginnings that major deviations may fester and grow. The *Hadeeths* mentioned in the texts have also been referenced to English translations of *Hadeeth* classics which are currently available, in order to facilitate further research for English speakers. This job was largely undertaken by brother Iftekhar Mackeen, to whom I am indeed grateful. In the case of *Fiqh* issues, I have not preferred any particular school of legal thought *(Madh-hab)*, but have instead endeavoured to follow the school which has the strongest support in the Qur'aan and *Sunnah*.

It should also be noted that although this series of texts was originally designed for the teaching of Islamic Studies in English medium high school and junior-high, it has also been prepared with new Muslim reverts in mind. Consequently, it is quite suited for courses in Islaam for English speaking adults. In fact, I have personally used them for a number of lecture series delivered to both Muslim reverts and Muslims by birth.

May Allaah accept these efforts to spread the knowledge of Islaam on an institutional level and bring it to fruition, as success lies ultimately in His hands alone.

Abu Ameenah Bilal Philips.
Riyadh, Saudi Arabia
1990 / 1411 A.H.

TRANSLITERATION

In order to provide the non-Arab with a more easily read set of symbols than those in current use, I have adopted a somewhat innovative system of transliteration particularly with regard to long vowels. It should be noted, however, that a very similar system was used by E. W. Lane in preparing his famous *Arabic-English Lexicon,* considered the most authoritative work in its field. Many other scholarly texts, written to teach Arabic pronunciation, also use similar systems. For example, Margaret K. Omar's *Saudi Arabic: Urban Hijazi Dialect,* (Washington, DC: Foreign Service Institute, 1975), as well as the Foreign Language Institute's *Saudi-Arabic: Headstart* (Monetery, CA: Defense Language Institute, 1980).

No transliteration can express exactly the vocalic differences between two languages nor can Roman characters give anything more than an approximate sound of the original Arabic words and phrases. There is also the difficulty of romanizing certain combinations of Arabic words which are pronounced differently from the written characters. Included in this category is the prefix *"al"* (representing the article "the"). When it precedes words beginning with letters known as *al-Huroof ash-Shamseeyah* (lit. solar letters), the sound of *"l"* is merged into the following letter; for example, *al-Rahmaan* is pronounced *ar-Rahmaan.* Whereas, in the case of all other letters, known as *al-Huroof al-Qamareeyah* (lit. lunar letters), the *"al"* is pronounced fully. I have followed the pronunciation for the facility of the average reader by writing *ar-Rahmaan* instead of *al-Rahmaan* and so on.

أ	a	ذ	dh
ب	b	ر	r
ت	t	ز	z
ث	th	س	s
ج	j	ش	sh
ح	h	ص	s
خ	kh	ض	d
د	d	ط	t

		Short Vowels	
ظ	dH		
ع	'	ـَ	a
غ	gh	ـِ	i
ف	f	ـُ	u
ق	q		
ك	k	**Long Vowels**	
ل	l	آ ـ ا	aa [2]
م	m	ي	ee
ن	n	و'	oo
ه	h		
ة	h/t	**Dipthongs**	
و	w	و'	aw
ي	y	ـَي	ay

Note:

Shaddah (ّ) The *Shaddah* is represented in Roman letters by doubled consonants. However, in actual pronunciation the letters should be merged and held briefly like the "n" sound produced by the *n/kn* combination in the word *unknown*, or the "n" in *unnerve*, the "b" in *grabbag*, the "t" in *freight-train*, the "r" in *overruled*, and "p" in *lamp post*, and the "d" in *mid-day*.

I have made an exception with (ّيِ), instead of *iyy*, I have used *eey* as in *Islaameeyah* because this more accurately conveys the sound.

---

[1] This *taa* has been commonly transliterated as "t" in all cases. However, such a system is not accurate and does not represent Arabic pronunciation.

[2] Thus, the Divine name (الله) commonly transliterated as Allah (pronounced as "ala" in "balance" by most English readers) is transliterated as Allaah throughout this book. In agreement with this principle Islam is transliterated Islaam.

1. TAWḤEED : SECTIONS

Literally *Tawheed* means to make something one or to call it one. In English when something is made one it is called a "unity". However, Islamically *Tawheed* means to believe that Allaah is the one and only God in all of the things that we do to please Him. For example, prayer should only be to Allaah, sacrifice should only be done in Allaah's name, charity should only be given for Allaah's pleasure and *Jihaad* should only be fought for the sake of Allaah's religion.

THE SECTIONS OF TAWḤEED

The subject of *Tawheed* has three sections.

(1) *Tawheed ar-Ruboobeeyah:* Unity of Lordship.

(2) *Tawheed al-Asmaa waṣ-Ṣifaat:* Unity of Allaah's Names and Attributes.

(3) *Tawheed al-'Ebaadah:* Unity of Worship.

1. Unity of Lordship

Tawheed ar-Ruboobeeyah means that we accept Allaah as being the only real power in the Universe. He caused all things to exist when there was nothing; thus, **He is called** اَلْخَالِقُ *al-Khaaliq*, the Creator. He is the one who gave all things the power to grow, to move **and to change, so He is called** *ar-Rabb* اَلرَّبُّ Nothing happens except what He allows to happen; thus He is called اَلْمَالِكُ *al-Maalik*, The Owner of The Universe.

When someone does evil, we recognize that it was Allaah who gave him a mind to think of evil, a body able to do it, and that it was by Allaah's permission that he was able to put his bad idea into practice. We should not say that Allaah caused him to do evil, because man chooses evil by himself. Instead, we should say that Allaah gave him the power to be able to think and do evil. He could not have done evil unless Allaah allowed it to happen, and he could not have thought to do evil unless Allaah gave him the ability to do so. But he chose to do evil by himself and Allaah let him to do it.

Allaah controls all that happens, good or bad, When we want to avoid some misfortune or get some good fortune, we should only turn to Allaah and seek his help. If we depend on created things which the common people call good luck charms, (like rabbit's feet and horse shoes)[1], to bring us good luck, we have destroyed this section of *Tawheed* by committing the biggest sin possible, known as *Shirk*. Similarly, if we fear created things which the common people believe will cause bad luck (like spilling salt, black cats crossing our paths, breaking mirrors, etc.)[2], thinking that we have saved ourselves from bad luck, we have also committed *Shirk* and destroyed this section of *Tawheed*.

---

[1] **The Rabbit's foot:** The hind paws of rabbits or gold and silver replicas of a hind paw are worn on chains and bracelets as good luck charms by millions in the West. The origin of this belief is based on the rabbit's habit of thumping their hind legs on the ground. According to the ancients, rabbits talked with the underground spirits when they thumped the ground. Hence, the paws were saved as a means of conveying one's wishes to the spirits as well as an instrument for bringing good luck in general.
Horseshoes: Many houses in America have horseshoes nailed over their doors, miniature versions are also worn on charm bracelets, key chains or necklaces, in the belief that they will bring good luck. The origin of this belief can be found in the ancient Greek mythology. In ancient Greece, horses were considered sacred animals. If a horse's shoe was hung over the door of a house, it was thought to bring good fortune. The open end of the horseshoe had to point upward, though, so it would hold the good luck. If it pointed downward, they believed that the good luck would spill out.

[2] **Spilling Salt:** If salt is spilled, many believe that misfortune will shortly follow, so the spilled salt is thrown over the left shoulder to counteract it. The origin of this omen lies in the ability of salt to keep things fresh. This was believed by the ancients to be due to its magical powers. Thus, spilling salt became a warning of evil. Since evil spirits were thought to live on one's left side, throwing the spilled salt over the left shoulder was supposed to satisfy the evil spirits.
Black cats: The crossing of a black cat in front of one's path signals the coming of =

2. Unity of Allaah's Names and Attributes

Tawheed al-Asmaa was-Sifaat means to describe Allaah according to the names and attributes by which He has described himself in the Qur'aan or by those used by Prophet Muḥammad (ﷺ) to describe Him. Because Allaah is the Greatest, His names are called *al-Asmaa al-Husnaa* (The Most Beautiful Names). Allaah said in the Qur'aan:

$$اَللَّهُ لَا إِلَهَ إِلَّا هُوَ لَهُ ٱلْأَسْمَآءُ ٱلْحُسْنَىٰ$$

"Allaah, there is no God but He. To Him belong the Most Beautiful names."

(Soorah Taa Haa (20): 8)

Everything which exists has attributes or qualities by which it is known. We learn in science that animals are different from plants due to certain attributes. Animals can move and the majority of them take care of their young, whereas plants do not have these characteristics.

Similarly, each of Allaah's names describes a certain attribute which only belongs to Him. For example, Allaah calls Himself اَلْأَوَّلُ *al-Awwal* The First, which means that before anything was, Allaah was. Nothing existed before Allaah, because Allaah created everything. A student may be called the first in the class or the first in a race, but he can not be the first before everything. Neither Allaah's names nor His attributes are the same as those of His creation. We should not give Allaah the attributes of His creation nor should we give the creation His attributes. Allaah has said in the Qur'aan:

= bad luck to many. This belief originated in the Middle Ages when people believed that black cats were witches' pets. Witches were supposed to make magic brews by mixing the brains of black cats with parts of toads, snakes and insects. If a witch's black cat lived for seven years, without ending up in a brew, the cat was supposed to change into a witch.

Breaking a Mirror: Many people believe that breaking a mirror accidentally is a sign of seven years of bad luck. Ancient people thought that their reflections in water were their souls. So if their reflections were shattered (e.g. if someone threw a pebble in the water), then their souls were also shattered. When mirrors were made this belief was transferred to them also.

$$\text{لَيْسَ كَمِثْلِهِ شَيْءٌ وَهُوَ السَّمِيعُ الْبَصِيرُ}$$

"There is nothing like Him and He sees and hears (all things)."

(Soorah ash-Shooraa (42):11)

In the Bible of the Christians and the Torah of the Jews they have written that Allaah spent the first six days creating the universe then He slept on the seventh. So they take either Saturday or Sunday as a day of rest in which work is looked at as a sin. However, by making Allaah like humans who tire from work and need rest, they have committed the biggest sin of *Shirk*. In the Qur'aan Allaah says:

$$\text{اللَّهُ لَا إِلَهَ إِلَّا هُوَ الْحَيُّ الْقَيُّومُ لَا تَأْخُذُهُ سِنَةٌ وَلَا نَوْمٌ}$$

"Allaah, there is no god besides Him. The Living, the Self-Subsisting. He does not become tired nor does He sleep."

(Soorah al-Baqarah (2):255)

3. Unity of Worship

Tawheed al-'Ebaadah means that we direct all of our prayers only to Allaah, because He is the only one who is able to answer our prayers. Some people say, if you want to complain to the director of schools, you as a student can not go directly to his office. You should speak to your teacher who will talk to the principal, who, in turn, will take your complaint to the director for you. In the same way, it is better to ask someone close to God, like the prophets or saints, to carry your prayers for you. Such a belief makes Allaah like humans who require intermediaries. However, Allaah is different, He hears and knows all things, so there is no need for anyone to carry our prayers to Allaah for us. Allaah has said in the Qur'aan:

$$\text{وَقَالَ رَبُّكُمُ ادْعُونِي أَسْتَجِبْ لَكُمْ}$$

"And your Lord said, 'Call on Me (in prayer) and I will answer you.' "

(Soorah Ghaafir (40):60)

Therefore, to pray to Prophet Muhammad (ﷺ) or other righteous people whom some people call "Saints," hoping that their prayers will reach Allaah and be answered through them is *Shirk,* the greatest of all sins.

It should be noted that worship in Islaam includes more than just our prayers. If we follow someone who makes *Halaal* (permissible) what Allaah has made *Haraam* or vice versa, we are also worshipping them. The proof of that is in a *Hadeeth* reported by 'Adee ibn Haatim that he heard the Prophet (ﷺ) recite the verse:

أَتَّخَذُوٓاْ أَحْبَارَهُمْ وَرُهْبَنَهُمْ أَرْبَابًا مِّن دُونِ ٱللَّهِ

"They have taken their Rabbis and Monks as lords along with Allaah."

(Soorah at-Tawbah: (9):31)

'Adee ibn Haatim said, "We didn't use to worship them." The Prophet (ﷺ) said: *"Did they not make **Haraam** what Allaah had made **Halaal**[1] and you all made it **Haraam,** and they made **Halaal** what Allaah had made **Haraam**[2] and you made it **Halaal**?"* He replied, "Certainly." The Prophet (ﷺ) then said *"That was your worship of them."*[3]

---

[1] Some Christian religious leaders forbade the marrying of more than one wife, marrying first cousins, priests marrying, and divorce.

[2] Some Christian leaders allowed the eating of pork, the drinking of alcohol, men marrying men, and making images of God and the Prophets.

[3] Collected by at-Tirmidhee and rated authentic *(Hasan)* by al-Albaanee in *Saheeh Sunan at-Tirmidhee,* vol. 3, p. 56, no. 2471).

QUESTIONS

1. Islamically *Tawheed* means to

   (a) make Allaah one of three gods.

   (b) believe that Allaah is one God in all that we do to please Him.

   (c) accept Allaah as the greatest of all gods and please Him in all that we do.

   (d) believe that Allaah is everything and everything is Allaah.

   (e) make man a unity.

2. Explain the meaning of *Tawheed ar-Ruboobeeyah?*

3. We should not say that Allaah caused someone to do evil because

   (a) Allaah made him do it.

   (b) nothing happens except what He allows to **happen.**

   (c) Allaah caused all things to exist.

   (d) he could not have thought to do evil unless Allaah gave him the ability to do so.

   (e) **man chooses evil by himself.**

4. *Tawheed ar-Ruboobeeyah* may be destroyed by

   (a) depending on created things to gain good luck.

   (b) saying that Allaah allows evil to take place.

   (c) believing that Allaah is the only real power in the universe.

   (d) believing that man chooses to do evil.

   (e) depending on Allaah in all matters.

5. *Tawheed al-Asmaa was Sifaat* means to

   (a) describe Allaah only in the way He and His Prophet (ﷺ) described Him.

(b) give Allaah the attributes of His creation.

(c) believe that Prophet Muhammad (ﷺ) possessed all of Allaah's attributes.

(d) give the creation Allaah's attributes.

(e) describe Allaah in human terms.

6. Explain the difference between Allaah's attribute of being One al-Ahad and a boy being number one in his class.

7. *Tawheed al-'Ebaadah* means

(a) to worship Prophet Muhammad (ﷺ) alone.

(b) that we only believe in Allaah.

(c) to worship Allaah alone.

(d) that we direct our prayers to Allaah through Prophet Muhammad (ﷺ).

(e) to believe that only Allaah created the universe.

8. Why is there no need for anyone to carry our prayers to Allaah?

9. Name and explain which section of *Tawheed* is destroyed by the following beliefs and practises:

(a) Making pictures of Allaah.

(b) Praying to the Prophet (ﷺ).

(c) The belief that Jesus is the son of God.

(d) Kissing the Qur'aan for good fortune.

(e) Believing that Allaah rested on the seventh day of creation.

(f) Wearing a Qur'aan on a chain for good fortune.

(g) Avoiding the number 13 believing that it is a source of bad luck.

(h) Asking a Saint (a dead righteous person) for protection or help.

(i) Saying stealing or cheating is *Halaal*.

2.   TAWḤEED: 'EBAADAH

THE PURPOSE OF CREATION

It is very important that we all understand the purpose for which we were created, otherwise we are likely to waste our time doing things which are of no real value. For example, if everyone were sent to school without knowing why they were sent there, they would probably all start playing and would continue to do so until someone told them why they were supposed to be there. Allaah, who is most wise, would not create us without a purpose, because anyone who does something without any reason behind it is considered unreasonable and foolish, and Allaah could never be that. For example, if a man made a machine which did not do anything, he would be looked at as being crazy. Or if someone came and knocked on a door, but when asked whom he wanted, he answered, 'I don't know' and when asked why he knocked, he again answered, 'I don't know.' Such an individual would be taken to the madhouse for treatment. A wise man is one who plans his affairs well in advance and does things for good reasons. Therefore, Allaah, the all-wise creator of man, must have created us for a very important purpose.

We all know that the purpose of our creation is not that obvious, otherwise everyone would be aware of it, and we would all be involved in doing similar things. Because our purpose is somewhat hidden, Allaah, Most Merciful, chose to reveal it to us by sending prophets with divine books containing the words of God. He could have sent angels with the message or revealed it by some other miraculous means and no one would be in any doubt about their purpose, but Allaah chose to send men to mankind in order to test their faith. He also sent along with these prophets certain miracles, to show the people that they were sent by Allaah. Allaah explained in the Qur'aan, the last book of revelation brought by the last Prophet (🖋), exactly what that purpose was. He said,

وَلَقَدۡ بَعَثۡنَا فِى كُلِّ أُمَّةٍ رَّسُولًا أَنِ ٱعۡبُدُواْ ٱللَّهَ

"Verily We have sent to every nation a messenger saying: Perform the *'Ebaadah* (worship) of Allaah."

(Naḥl (16):37).

He also said,

وَمَا خَلَقۡتُ ٱلۡجِنَّ وَٱلۡإِنسَ إِلَّا لِيَعۡبُدُونِ

"I only created the *Jinn* and mankind for My *'Ebaadah*."

(Soorah adh-Dhaariyaat (51):57).

Therefore our purpose in life is the *'Ebaadah* of Allaah.

Definition

If we are to perform Allaah's *'Ebaadah* properly, we must know exactly what it is and what it is not. *'Ebaadah* is often translated into English as "worship", which is defined as: honour and respect mixed with love and fear toward God, a god or a sacred object. In Arabic *'Ebaadah* literally means: subservience (i.e. the willingness to serve in a low position) as well as submission (i.e. the surrender of one's self or rights). It comes from the word *'Abd* which means "slave or servant".

Islamically *'Ebaadah* is to obey Allaah by doing whatever He has commanded and by avoiding whatever He has forbidden. This form of obedience is called *'Ebaadah*, because it involves serving God and surrendering (giving up) one's will to God's will. This is why the best name a Muslim man can take is *'Abd Allaah* ('Abdullaah), that is, slave or servant of Allaah. Perhaps the best name for a Muslim woman is *Amah Allaah* (Amatullaah: female slave or servant of Allaah). Ibn 'Umar reported that Allaah's Messenger (ﷺ) said, *"Verily, the most beloved of your names to Allaah, Most Great and Glorious, are 'Abdullaah and 'AbdurRahmaan."*[1] The Prophet (ﷺ) also prefer-

---

[1] Collected by Muslim *(Sahih Muslim* (English Trans.), vol. 3, p. 1188, no. 5315) and Abu Daawood *(Sunan Abu Dawud* (English Trans.), vol. 3, p. 1377, no. 4931).

red the name *'Abd* in reference to himself saying, *"Do not exaggerate your praise of me the way the Christians did to Jesus the son of Mary, for verily I'm only a slave ('Abd) so refer to me as 'Abd of Allaah and His Messenger."*[1]

'Ebaadah is the core of Islaam because the word "Islaam" means the surrender of one's will to Allaah, which is the highest level of obedience that one can reach. Our physical bodies obey Allaah's laws, commonly called the "laws of nature", without any choice. Therefore, our bodies can be considered Muslims, in submission to Allaah like the rest of creation. But our minds, which are run by our souls, have the ability to choose to submit to Allaah's social and spiritual laws or not. When we make the mental choice to put our souls in line with the rest of creation by accepting Allaah's supremacy, we then become Muslims in the full sense of the word. That choice is expressed in two particular ways:

1. In the words of the declaration of faith (The *Shahaadah*):

   "Laa elaaha illal-laah"
   There is nothing worthy of our *'Ebaadah* except Allaah,
   and

   "Muhammadur-Rasoolullaah"
   Muhammad (🕌) is the Prophet of Allaah.

2. In the acts obedience or *'Ebaadah*, e.g. *Salaah, Zakaah, Sawm,* and *Hajj*.

Since Islaam covers all areas of life, every act in a Muslim's life can become an act of *'Ebaadah*. If he obeys Allaah's laws in all the areas of his life by living according to the way of the Prophet (🕌), then even the simplest of acts can become *'Ebaadah*. For example, if one begins his daily meals with the short prayer: *Bismillaah* (In the name

---

[1] Collected by al-Bukhaaree *(Sahih Al-Bukhari* (Arabic-English), vol. 4, p. 435, no. 654) and Muslim.

of Allaah); eats and drinks with only his right hand; avoids using gold or silver utensils; avoids over-eating by eating a third, drinking a third and leaving a third for breathing; and ends his meal with the short prayer: al-Ḥamdulil-laah (all praise is Allaah's), the everyday act of eating becomes an act of worship and submission to Allaah for which he will be rewarded.

The Khaleefah

Therefore, if we are to fulfill our purpose in this life, we have to find out what Allaah wants from us in all areas of our lives. After finding out what is required of us, we then have to put that knowledge into practice so that it may result in righteous deeds. If our lives become in a state of harmony with Allaah's laws, we then become higher and more noble than all of creation. Even the angels who never disobey Allaah, will be on a lower level than us. This is the meaning of Allaah's command to the angels to bow down to prophet Aadam

وَإِذْ قُلْنَا لِلْمَلَٰٓئِكَةِ ٱسْجُدُوا۟ لِءَادَمَ فَسَجَدُوٓا۟ إِلَّآ إِبْلِيسَ

"And when We told the angels to prostrate to Adam, they all prostrated except Iblees."

(Soorah al-Baqarah (2):34).

This was Allaah's way of showing that man was created to be on a higher level than the angels and the rest of creation. Iblees, the *Jinn*, who was among the angels realized this and refused to prostrate to Aadam. When Allaah asked him why he did not bow down, he replied,

قَالَ أَنَا۠ خَيْرٌ مِّنْهُ خَلَقْتَنِى مِن نَّارٍ وَخَلَقْتَهُۥ مِن طِينٍ

"I am better than him. You created me from fire and created him from clay."

(Soorah al-A'raaf (7):12).

If we reach the higher levels of submission through sincere *'Ebaadah*, we fulfill the role of *Khaleefah*, who is responsible for governing the inhabitants of the earth, and maintaining law and order among all living and non-living beings. This is the purpose of man's creation in relation to the rest of creation. This state is the fulfillment of Allaah's statement,

وَإِذْ قَالَ رَبُّكَ لِلْمَلَٰٓئِكَةِ إِنِّي جَاعِلٌ فِي ٱلْأَرْضِ خَلِيفَةً

"And when We informed the Angels saying: Verily I will place on earth a *Khaleefah*."

(Soorah Baqarah (2):30).

If, on the other hand, we refuse to make our lives conform to Allaah's laws and rebel like Iblees, we become lower than the lowest of creation. That is what Allaah meant when He described those who went against His laws saying,

إِنْ هُمْ إِلَّا كَٱلْأَنْعَٰمِ بَلْ هُمْ أَضَلُّ سَبِيلًا

"Verily they are like cattle, nay, they are even more lost from the path."

(Soorah al-Furqaan (25):44)

Those who have no fear of God sometimes hunt animals for sport until they have wiped out whole species of animals. On the other hand, animals only hunt and kill other animals out of need. Islaam teaches that it is forbidden to kill animals for fun and sport. Similarly, those industrial companies whose only goal is profit, release many dangerous chemicals into the environment, destroying lakes, rivers and forests all around the world. One never finds animals carelessly destroying the environment. Islaam forbids the destruction of the environment even during wars, and encourages the planting of trees and the protection of rivers, lakes and seas.

QUESTIONS

1. (a) Why is it important to understand the purpose of our creation?

   (b) Explain why must there be a purpose for our creation?

   (c) How do we know that the purpose in life is not obvious?

   (d) What is the purpose of our creation?

2. The Islamic definition of *'Ebaadah* is
   (a) worship.
   (b) slave or servant.
   (c) the willingness to serve in a low position.
   (d) to obey Allaah by doing whatever He has commanded and by avoiding whatever He has forbidden.
   (e) obedience to the laws of nature.

3. Why is *'Ebaadah* considered the "core" of Islaam?

4. The most beloved of our names to Allaah is
   (a) Muhammad.
   (b) Ahmad.
   (c) 'Abdul-Waahid.
   (d) 'Abdullaah.
   (e) 'Ubaadah.

5. All created things are considered to be Muslims because
   (a) they all obey Allaah's laws of nature.
   (b) they all chose to obey Allaah's laws.
   (c) everything declares its faith in Allaah.
   (d) Allaah does not create anything with a purpose.
   (e) Allaah made the angels bow down to Aadam.

6. How can the whole life of a Muslim become *'Ebaadah?*

7. Allaah's command to the angels to bow down to Aadam meant

   (a) that the angels were created to worship man.
   (b) all men are superior to angels.

(c) that humans who want to obey Allaah's laws should worship angels.

(d) that man was created to be on a higher level than the angels.

(e) we must all bow down to Aadam.

8. What is man's purpose in relation to the rest of creation?

9. Explain what happens when a man refuses to follow Allaah's laws. Give an example to support your answer?

3. TAWHEED: ISRAA' AND MI'RAAJ

Israa' literally means a journey by night and *Mi'raaj* literally means an elevator, i.e., an instrument which lifts something up. But, in Islaam, *Israa'* refers to a miraculous night-journey made by the last Prophet (ﷺ) from Makkah to Jerusalem, and *Mi'raaj* refers to the vehicle which took the Prophet (ﷺ) from Jerusalem, up and out of the universe, through the seven heavens, and into the direct presence of Allaah.

The Night Journey *(Israa')*

Towards the end of a calm night, one year before the *Hijrah*, the roof of the Prophet Muhammad's (ﷺ) house split open and angel Jibreel (Gabriel) descended into the Prophet's (ﷺ) room. He went over to the Prophet (ﷺ), opened his shirt and cut open his chest. He then removed his heart and washed its inside with *ZamZam* water. After he had completed washing it, he then brought a gold dish filled with *Eemaan* (faith) and *Hikmah* (wisdom),[1] emptied it into the Prophet's (ﷺ) chest and then closed it all up.[2] Jibreel then nudged the Prophet (ﷺ) until he awoke. When the Prophet (ﷺ) got up, Jibreel took a hold of his hand and lead him outside of his house to the gate of *Ka'bah*. There the Prophet (ﷺ) found a strange unearthly animal. It was smaller than a mule but larger than a donkey, white in color and having a wing on either of its hind legs. He was informed that its name was "*Buraaq*", a name taken from the Arabic word *Barq* which means a flash of lightning. Jibreel helped the Prophet (ﷺ) mount it and they set off to the north. Each stride of the *Buraaq* took it to the horizon, and, in no time they reached Jerusalem. There the Prophet (ﷺ) dismounted and tied the animal to the same ring on the door of al-Masjid *al-Aqsaa* used by the prophets. The

---

[1] Wisdom.

[2] Reported by Anas Ibn Maalik and Abu Dharr and collected by al-Bukhaaree *(Sahih Al-Bukhari* (Arabic-English), vol. 9, pp. 449-450, no. 605) and Muslim *(Sahih Muslim* (English Trans.), vol. 1, pp. 103-4, no. 313).

Prophet (ﷺ) entered the masjid and prayed two *Rak'ahs*. When he finished the noticed a group of other prophets also making *Salaah* there. He saw among them Prophet Moosaa, Prophet 'Eesaa and Prophet Ibraaheem. Prophet Muhammad (ﷺ) was then told to lead them all in *Salaah*. When the Prophet (ﷺ) finished this *Salaah*, someone said to him, "This is Maalik, the guardian of the Hellfire, so give him *Salaams*." When he turned around to greet him, the angel gave him *Salaams* before he had time to do so.[1]

Jibreel then brought two vessels and presented them to the Prophet (ﷺ). One was filled with wine and the other filled with milk. The Prophet (ﷺ) chose the vessel filled with milk and drank from it. Jibreel then said, "You have been guided to the *Fitrah*."[2]

The Ascent *(Mi'raaj)*

The Prophet (ﷺ) then left the masjid and the *Mi'raaj* was brought for him. Jibreel helped him get into it, and it shot up into the heavens and out of the solar system. Travelling at a tremendous rate, the Prophet (ﷺ) and Jibreel soon left our galaxy and raced past the other galaxies until they reached the end of the universe. At the end of the universe, they arrived at the boundary of the lowest heaven. Jibreel then requested that its gate be opened for them. Jibreel was then asked who he was and who was with him. When he informed the guardian angel who they were, he was then asked if the Prophet (ﷺ) had been sent for. When he said that that was so, the guardian said, "Welcome! His coming is good," and the gate was opened. When they went into the lowest heaven the Prophet (ﷺ) saw a man sitting with a large group of people on his right and a large group on his left. When the man looked at those on his right he laughed, and when he looked at those on his left he wept. The Prophet (ﷺ)

---

[1] Reported by Abu Hurayrah and collected by Muslim *(Sahih Muslim* (English Trans.), vol. 1, p. 110, no. 328).

[2] Reported by Abu Hurayrah and collected by Muslim *(Sahih Muslim* (English Trans.), vol. 1, p. 108 no. 322).

asked Jibreel who the man was and Jibreel replied, "This is your father Aadam, so greet him." When the Prophet (ﷺ) did so, Prophet Aadam returned his *Salaams* and said, "Welcome! Oh good son and good Prophet." Jibreel then said, "These people on his right and left are the souls of his descendants. Those of them on his left are the inhabitants of Hell, so when he looks on his right side he laughs and when he looks on his left he cries." Jibreel then took him up to the second heaven where he met and greeted Prophets 'Eesaa and Yahyaa, up to the third where he met and greeted Prophet Yousuf; up to the fourth where he met and greeted Prophet Idrees, up to the fifth where he met and greeted Prophet Haaroon, and up to the sixth where he met Prophet Moosaa. When he went on past Prophet Moosaa, Moosaa wept, and when he was asked why he wept he replied, 'I am crying because more followers of a young man, who was sent as a prophet after my time, will enter paradise than my followers.' He then went on up with Jibreel to the seventh heaven, requested entrance and they came upon Prophet Ibraaheem leaning with his back against the house of worship called *al-Bayt al-Ma'moor*.[1] Prophet Muhammad (ﷺ) observed approximately seventy thousand angels, entering this heavenly house of worship without seeing any of them leave. Jibreel then led the Prophet (ﷺ) to the lote-tree of the boundary, which he described as having leaves like the ears of elephants and fruits like large earthen-ware jugs. The lote-tree marked the spot, beyond which even Jibreel could not go, but Allaah permitted the Prophet Muhammad (ﷺ) to go beyond it and spoke to him directly. Allaah revealed to the Prophet (ﷺ) the last verses of Soorah al-Baqarah and promised him that the major sins of his followers would be forgiven if they did not commit *Shirk*. Allaah also made *Salaah* compulsory fifty times per day for the Prophet (ﷺ) and his followers. On the Prophet's (ﷺ) return he passed by Prophet Moosaa who asked him what worship had been prescribed

---

[1] It is a house of worship in the heavens used by the angels after which the *Ka'bah* was designed.

for him. When the Prophet (ﷺ) informed him, Moosaa said, "Your people are not capable of doing fifty daily prayers. I swear by Allaah that I have tested men before your time and tried my best with the Israelites, so go back to your Lord and ask Him to make things lighter for your people." The Prophet (ﷺ) did so and Allaah reduced it by ten, but Moosaa suggested that he return and request a further reduction for the same reason, so he returned. The Prophet (ﷺ) continued going back and forth between his Lord and Moosaa until Allaah said, "They are five prayers everyday, Muhammad, each being rewarded as ten, so that makes fifty times of prayer. He who intends to do a good deed and does not do it will have a good deed recorded for him, and if he does it, it will be recorded for him as ten; whereas, he who intends to do an evil deed and does not do it will have nothing recorded against him, and if he does it, only one evil deed will be recorded against him." When he came down and Moosaa told him to go back, he replied, "I have asked my Lord till I am ashamed to face Him. I am now satisfied and I submit."[1] The Prophet (ﷺ) was then taken into Paradise and he reported that he saw in it domes of pearls and that its soil was made of musk.[2] He was also taken to Hell and Allaah showed him scenes from the future. He saw in the Hellfire people receiving terrible punishments for various sins. The Prophet (ﷺ) then took the Mi'raaj and descended with Jibreel to al-Masjid al-Aqsaa. From there he mounted the Buraaq and returned to his home in Makkah where he found his bed still warm.

The Return

The following morning, the Prophet (ﷺ) went to the Quraysh's tribal meeting place, and when Abu Jahl came up to him, he informed

---

[1] Reported by Anas ibn Maalik and collected by al-Bukhaaree (Sahih Al-Bukhari (Arabic-English), vol. 9, pp. 449-54, no. 608).

[2] Reported by Ibn Hazm and Anas and collected by al-Bukhaaree (Sahih Al-Bukhari (Arabic-English), vol. 9, pp. 449-54, no. 608) and Muslim (Sahih Muslim (English Trans.), vol. 1, pp. 103-4, no. 313).

him of his journey. Abu Jahl then called all the people to hear the Prophet's (ﷺ) story, and when he related it to them, they stared at him in amazement and disbelief. Some Muslim converts whose *Eemaan* was weak left Islaam and returned to *Kufr*, because of the incredible tale which the Prophet (ﷺ) had told.

Some of the people ran to Abu Bakr and told him that his companion, Muhammad (ﷺ), claimed that he went to Jerusalem, made *Salaah* there, and returned to Makkah in one night. Abu Bakr told them that they were lying about the Prophet (ﷺ), because the story was too strange, but they told him that the Prophet (ﷺ) was at the Ka'bah telling it to the people. When they told him that, they were sure that he would also leave Islaam, because it was obvious to them that Muhammad (ﷺ) must be lying. But Abu Bakr told them, "By Allaah, if he actually said that, he has told the truth. There really is nothing to be amazed about, for he has told me that information comes to him from Allaah, from the sky to the earth, in an instant during the night or day and I believe him. And that is even more strange." Because of that statement of Abu Bakr, the Prophet (ﷺ) gave him the title of *"as-Siddeeq* (the truthful)."

The people then demanded from the Prophet (ﷺ) proof of what he said. They knew that he had never travelled to Jerusalem, so some of them demanded that he describe it. The Prophet (ﷺ) became worried, as he had forgotton most of its details. He had only been there at night and had not paid much attention to its details. But, Allaah blessed him with a vision in which he saw Jerusalem as if he were there. So he was able to describe even its smallest details for them.[1] For the others, he told them that on his way to Jerusalem he passed by a stray camel belonging to one of the clans which had camped in a valley. It had escaped from a group of them and he lead them to it. He also told them that on his return he passed by the same clan's caravan and found them all sleeping. They had a drinking vessel with some water

---

[1] Reported by Jaabir and collected by al-Bukhaaree and Muslim *(Sahih Muslim* (English Trans.), vol. 1, p. 104, no. 326).

in it which they had covered, so he uncovered it, drank its contents and put the cover back on the same way it was. He then informed them that the caravan was on its way to Makkah and he further described its lead camel. So the people rushed out to meet the caravan and found it as he had described it. They then asked the clan about the stray camel and the drinking vessel, and they'replied, "By Allaah! He told the truth, we had camped in the valley which he mentioned and one of our camels had run off. We heard a man's voice calling us to it until we caught it." They also mentioned that they had left water in their jug and were surprised to find that it was all gone the next morning.

THE SIGNIFICANCE OF MI'RAAJ

Strengthening the Prophethood

a) Shortly before the   *Hijrah*, (the migration to Madeenah) the Prophet's uncle Abu Taalib died. Though the Prophet (ﷺ) tried his best to get him to accept Islaam, he chose to remain in the religion of his forefathers. This hurt the Prophet (ﷺ) a lot because Abu Taalib had raised him from his early childhood and had protected him from a lot of the harm which the tribe of Quraysh had tried to do to him. So Abu Taalib's death affected the Prophet (ﷺ) in two ways: (1) He did not join Islaam and (2) He could no longer shield the Prophet (ﷺ) from the anger of the Quraysh.

b) Three days after Abu Taalib's death, the Prophet's wife, Khadeejah bint Khuwaylid died. It was she who comforted him during his first difficult experiences with revelation and during the early attacks and rejection of his people.

c) Following that, the Prophet (ﷺ) went to Taa'if in the hope of spreading Islaam there, but his invitation to Islaam was totally rejected. He was chased out of the city and stoned so badly that his sandals became clogged with blood.

From these events which occurred around the same time we can see that the Prophet (ﷺ) had suffered a series of disappointing setbacks and trials. Thus, Allaah took him up into His presence in order to strengthen him spiritually and prepare him for the next difficult stage of prophethood which was to come.

THE SIGNIFICANCE OF ISRAA'

Proof of the Prophethood

The miraculous night journey of the Prophet (ﷺ) provided him with additional proof to show his people that he had been sent by Allaah. It would not have been possible to prove his prophethood to the people by describing his trip into the heavens, as it was something none of them had experienced. It would have only sounded to them like a dream or just a wild story. But some of them had been to Jerusalem, and they all could ask the caravan to confirm his claims. So, his accurate description of the temple *(al-Masjid al-Aqsaa)* and its surroundings in detail, as well as the lost camel and the emptying of the drinking vessel proved to them, without a shadow of a doubt, that he was a prophet from Allaah.

LESSONS FROM ISRAA' AND MI'RAAJ

1. Allaah is Above Creation

The events of that miraculous journey of the Prophet (ﷺ) up through the heavens to the direct presence of Allaah, indirectly confirm the fact that Allaah is not inside His creation. It shows that He is not a part of His creation nor is He surrounded by His creation, instead He is above His creation. For, if He was everywhere as some people claim, the Prophet (ﷺ) would not have needed to even leave his room in order to be in the direct presence of Allaah. However, Allaah sees and hears all things and nothing at all is hidden from Him. His knowledge is everywhere, but there is no need for Him to be everywhere. In the same way that we are able to sit in our living-rooms and watch on T.V. what is going on half-way around the world without having to be there, Allaah knows all things without having to be in all places.

2. Allaah Can Not Be Seen in This Life

When the Prophet (ﷺ) was asked whether he saw Allaah during his journey in the *Mir'aaj,* he replied, *"There was only light, how could I see Him?"*[1] The fact that Prophet Muhammad (ﷺ) could not see Allaah, just as Prophet Moses before him was unable to see Him, shows that no man can see Allaah in this life. Therefore, we know with certainty that all those who claim to have seen Allaah are either purposely lying for fame and honor or they have been tricked by Satan into believing that they have seen Him.

3. Salaah : The Greatest Pillar Of Islaam

Salaah was the first act of worship which Allaah made compulsory on Muslims and it was the only one which He ordered in Makkah. All the other pillars of Islaam were made obligatory in Madeenah, after the *Hijrah.* This pillar is so important that Allaah chose to reveal it when He spoke directly to the Prophet (ﷺ) above the heavens.

---

[1] Reported by Abu Dharr and collected by Muslim *(Sahih Muslim* (English Trans.), vol. 1, p. 113, no. 341).

QUESTIONS

1. *Israa'* literally means
   (a) an elevator.
   (b) lightning.
   (c) the lote tree of the Boundary.
   (d) the miraculous journey of the Prophet (ﷺ) from Makkah to Madeenah.
   (e) a journey by night.

2. Islamically *Mi'raaj* refers to
   (a) a journey by night.
   (b) a vehicle smaller than a mule with a wing on each hind leg.
   (c) the vehicle which took the Prophet (ﷺ) into the heavens.
   (d) lightning.
   (e) an elevator.

3. How was the Prophet (ﷺ) prepared for his journey into the heavens?

4. The *Buraaq* was
   (a) an unearthly animal which the Prophet (ﷺ) rode from Makkah to Jerusalem and back.
   (b) a bolt of lightning which the Prophet (ﷺ) saw during *Mi'raaj*.
   (c) the vehicle which Jibreel rode from Makkah to Jerusalem.
   (d) the house in the heavens which the Prophet (ﷺ) saw filled with angels.
   (e) a donkey with wings on its front legs.

5. What was the purpose of the lote tree of the boundary?

6. What are the two things which were revealed to the Prophet (ﷺ) in the seventh heaven?
   (a) The first two verses of Soorah al-Baqarah.
   (b) *Zakaah* and fasting in Ramadaan.
   (c) *'Eed Salaah* and the last chapters of the Qur'aan.
   (d) The last verses of Soorah al-Baqarah and *Salaah*.
   (e) The *Buraaq* and the Lote tree of the Boundary.

7. (a) Why did the Prophet (ﷺ) give Abu Bakr the name *as-Ṣid-deeq?*
   (b) Briefly explain why some people left Islaam on learning about the Prophet's night journey?
   (c) Describe two incidents from the *Israa'* which proved to the Makkans that the Prophet's journey was true.

8. The main importance of *Mi'raaj* to the Prophet (ﷺ) was that it
   (a) provided clear proof of the prophethood to the pagan Makkans.
   (b) confirmed Allaah's oneness to the Prophet's (ﷺ) followers.
   (c) strengthened the Prophethood.
   (d) confirmed the existence of the seven heavens.
   (e) made *Salaah* compulsory fifty times per day.

9. The main significance of *Israa'* was that it
   (a) strengthened Prophet Muhammad's (ﷺ) prophethood.
   (b) confirmed for the Prophet (ﷺ) that he was a Prophet of God.
   (c) clearly proved the truth of Muhammad's (ﷺ) prophethood to the pagans of Makkah.
   (d) provided proof that Allaah is above His creation.
   (e) established the existence of the *Buraaq.*

10. Briefly mention the three lessons which may be learned from *Israa'* and *Mi'raaj.*

4. USOOL AT-TAFSEER

THE COLLECTION OF THE QUR'AAN

The Arabic word *Usool* is the plural of *Asl* which means "foundation, base or origin", and *Tafseer* is used to mean "explanation of the Qur'aan". So, *Usool at-Tafseer* means the fundamental pieces of knowledge needed to help in the understanding of the Qur'aan. In this section on the Fundamentals of *Tafseer (Usool at-Tafseer)*, we will look at how the Qur'aan was written and compiled into one book, as well as the significance of that knowledge.

A. THE ERA OF THE PROPHET(ﷺ) 609-632 C.E.[1]

The Qur'aan was revealed to Prophet Muhammad (ﷺ) in sections throughout the twenty-three years of his prophethood. Whenever a problem arose or whenever Allaah wanted to give the Prophet (ﷺ) and his followers special advice, Allaah would send angel Jibreel with a part of the Qur'aan which he would recite to the Prophet (ﷺ). Thus, the Qur'aan was not revealed all at once in its complete form, like the earlier books of revelation, but in parts over a period of time.

Preservation of the Qur'aan

When Jibreel first recited a part of the Qur'aan to the Prophet (ﷺ), the Prophet (ﷺ) tried to repeat it after him, word for word. Allaah later had Jibreel tell him not to do so. He was told instead to listen to the Qur'aan carefully. When the Prophet (ﷺ) did that Allaah caused him to be able to remember everything without any effort on his part.

Allaah said in the Qur'aan:

---

[1] C.E. (i.e. Christian Era) is used instead of **A.D.** *(Anno Domini,* lit. in the year of our Lord) because Muslims do not recognize Jesus, the son of Mary, as the Lord, but as a Prophet of the Lord God.

"Do not move your tongue to hastily (learn) it. Surely we will collect it and recite it. So, when we recite it, follow its recital."

(Soorah al-Qiyaamah (75):16-18)

It was very important that the Prophet (ﷺ) remember all that was revealed to him, because he could neither read nor write.

The Prophet (ﷺ) passed on all of the Qur'aan to his companions before he died. He used a number of different ways to make sure that they memorized and recorded it exactly as he learned it.

1. The Prophet (ﷺ) used to recite aloud various parts of the Qur'aan in the *Salaahs* (Congregational Prayers). In that way, his followers used to hear parts of the Qur'aan daily.

2. Everyone who entered Islaam would be taught parts of the Qur'aan which they would have to use in their daily prayers. Thus, Muslims were always learning or teaching various parts of the Qur'aan.

3. The Prophet (ﷺ) informed his followers that the best of them were those who learned and taught the Qur'aan. This encouraged them to make even greater efforts to memorize the Qur'aan and teach it to others.

4. Those who were able to read and write were told by the Prophet (ﷺ) to write down the various sections of the Qur'aan as they were revealed. The Prophet (ﷺ) would tell them the order in which they should record the verses.

Because there was no paper in Arabia at that time, the Qur'aan was written down on anything which was available. The companions wrote the verses of Qur'aan on date palm leaves, flat stones, tree bark, wood, dried animal skins and even the shoulder blades of sheep or camels. Thus, the verses of the Qur'aan were preserved in the hearts of the Muslims, as well as written down, during the lifetime of the Prophet (ﷺ). Since people entered Islaam at various points during the Prophet's (ﷺ) mission, only a few of them heard all of the Qur'aan directly from the Prophet (ﷺ). Also some companions were able to memorize better than others. So, even though all of them memorized portions of the Qur'aan, only a few were able to memorize all of the Qur'aan during the Prophet's (ﷺ) lifetime.

When the Prophet (ﷺ) died in the year 632 C.E., the whole of the Qur'aan was not written down in one complete book. It was recorded on various pieces of writing material and kept in the possession of different followers of the Prophet (ﷺ). Each had sections but none of them had all. Because of the fact that the verses of the Qur'aan continued to be revealed up until a few months before the Prophet's (ﷺ) death, the companions were more concerned with recording and memorizing it than putting it all together in one book. Consequently, the gathering of the Qur'aan into one text was not done during the Prophet's (ﷺ) lifetime.

B.   THE ERA OF ABU BAKR   632-634 C.E.

After the death of the Prophet (ﷺ), there arose three main groups opposed to Islaam in the Arabian peninsula.

1. The first group was made up of those who decided that they did not want to pay the Islamic tax, *Zakaah,* to anyone other than the Prophet (ﷺ). They did not feel that *Zakaah* was a pillar of Islaam just like *Salaah, Sawm* and *Hajj.* They instead looked at *Zakaah* as tribute; a kind of tax paid to the one who conquered them. So, when the Prophet (ﷺ) died, they felt that they were no longer required to pay it. When Abu Bakr became the leader of the Muslim state, this group refused to pay the *Zakaah* and sent armies to the capital, Madeenah, in order to topple the Muslim state. They demanded to be excused from paying *Zakaah* or else they would attack and destroy the centers of Islaam.

2. The first group was joined by those who had entered Islaam in order to escape defeat, as well as those who simply wanted to be on

the winning side. This group did not believe in Allaah and His Messenger at all. They wanted to destroy Islaam so they could be free to do whatever they wanted to do. Since the armies of those who refused to pay *Zakaah* appeared strong, many of these hypocrites joined them.

3. The third group was the false prophets and prophetesses. In the Najd, in the region of Yamaamah, an Arab from the tribe of Haneefah called Musaylimah claimed prophethood. In the southern part of Arabia, another Arab from the tribe of 'Ans called al-Aswad, claimed prophethood and took over Najraan. To the north of Arabia an Arab woman called Sajaah from the Tameem tribe also claimed prophethood and rose in arms against the Muslim state. These false prophets all invited people to leave Islaam by claiming that Allaah had revealed to them new laws making allowable most of the things which were forbidden by Prophet Muhammad (ﷺ).

True Muslims under the leadership of Caliph Abu Bakr, were forced to fight these three groups in order to re-establish Islaam throughout the Arabian peninsula.

The First Writing

During these wars known as the *Riddah* (apostasy), many of those who had memorized large portions of the Qur'aan were killed. Those Muslims who had a lot of Qur'aan in their hearts knew well the rewards which Allaah has promised those who fight for Islaam. So, they would always be in the front lines of all the battles.

'Umar ibn al-Khattaab realized the danger of what was happening and feared that if something was not done immediately, the Qur'aan would be lost to future generations of Muslims. So he went to Caliph Abu Bakr and advised him to have the whole Qur'aan written down in one book in order to preserve it from being lost. Abu Bakr at first refused to do so, because the Prophet (ﷺ) had not told them to do it. He was afraid of bringing anything new into the religion because the Prophet (ﷺ) had warned them about changing the religion. Christians had gone astray before them because they changed the religion which Prophet 'Eesaa brought after he left them. So Abu Bakr was very much against making any changes in the religion which Prophet Muḥammad (ﷺ) had not told them to do. However, after thinking over the situation very carefully, he came to realize that 'Umar's advice was right and that it was not really a change in the religion. The Prophet (ﷺ) had ordered them to write down the various verses and chapters of the Qur'aan, while it was being revealed, in order to help preserve it. Compiling all of what was written into one complete book was then only the completion of what the Prophet (ﷺ) had begun.

Caliph Abu Bakr asked Zayd ibn Thaabit to be in charge of collecting and writing down the whole Qur'aan. Zayd at first refused to do it for the same reasons that Abu Bakr had, but after some time he also came to realize that it was right. Zayd was chosen because he was:

1) One of the best reciters of the Qur'aan.

2) One of the few who had memorized the whole Qur'aan during the Prophet's (ﷺ) lifetime.

3) One of those whom the Prophet (ﷺ) asked to write down the Qur'aan.

4) One of the few who were present when the Prophet (ﷺ) recited the whole Qur'aan during the last Ramadaan of his life.

Zayd began the process by collecting all of the materials on which the Qur'aan had been written. He then gathered around him all of those who had also memorized all of the Qur'aan or large portions of it. He then compared what was written down with what he and others had memorized. If all agreed, he would then write it down on pages of leather. In this way the whole Qur'aan was written down during the reign of the first Caliph. On its completion, Zayd turned it over to Caliph Abu Bakr who kept it until his death, two years after he had become Caliph.

Just before his death, Abu Bakr turned over the Qur'aan to 'Umar whom he had chosen to be the second Caliph. 'Umar kept this copy of the Qur'aan with him until his death, ten years later, at the hand of an assassin named Abu Lu'lu'. The Qur'aan was then turned over to his daughter, Hafsah, who was also one of the Prophet's (ﷺ) wives. Hafsah kept the Qur'aan in her house in al-Madeenah, but she made it available to anyone who wanted to make copies from it, or check the accuracy of what they had memorized.

C. THE ERA OF 'UTHMAAN 644-656 C.E.

After the death of the second Caliph, 'Umar, a committee made up of six of the most famous companions of the Prophet (ﷺ) chose 'Uthmaan ibn 'Affaan to be the third Caliph.

During the reign of Caliph 'Umar (634-644 C.E.), the Islamic state expanded beyond the borders of the Arabian peninsula into Egypt, Syria and Iraq. In the subsequent reign of Caliph 'Uthmaan, the expansion continued on into Persia, India, Russia, China, Turkey and across North Africa. Many of the people of these regions accepted Islaam and learned the recitation of Qur'aan from the early Muslims. The Qur'aan was revealed to the Prophet (ﷺ) in seven different Arabic dialects, and the early Muslims taught the Qur'aan in its different readings.

The Second Writing

In the Muslim provinces, some Arabs began to boast that their dialect was superior to that of others. Also, when new Muslims made mistakes in their recitation of the Qur'aan, it was sometimes difficult to tell whether it was really an error or whether it was one of the seven readings which were taught by the Prophet (ﷺ). These problems eventually became a source of confusion in the Muslim provinces outside of Arabia. One of the prophet's companions *(Sahaabah)* by the name of Hudhayfah ibn al-Yamaan noticed the confusion while he was in Iraq, and feared that it might lead to a breakup of the Muslim nation and the changing of the Qur'aan. On his return to the capital, he informed Caliph 'Uthmaan of what he had heard and seen. Caliph

'Uthmaan realized the seriousness of the situation and called the major *Sahaabah* together in order to find a solution to the problem. They decided to make official copies of the Qur'aan from the one compiled in Caliph Abu Bakr's time and limit the people to its recitation.

'Uthmaan asked Hafsah for the original copy of the Qur'aan and called on Zayd ibn Thaabit to head a committee of four Qur'anic scholars who would take on the task of making the official copies. When the copies were completed, the original was returned to Hafsah. A total of seven copies were made and one was sent to Makkah, another to Syria, one to Basrah, one to Kufah, one to Yemen, one to Bahrain and one was kept in the capital, al-Madeenah. Caliph 'Uthmaan sent an official reciter of the Qur'aan with each copy in order to clear up any problems which might later arise. He also ordered that all other copies of the Qur'aan be destroyed, as people had made notes in their personal copies and some copies were incomplete. All new copies were then made from the official copy called *Mus-haf Uthmaan,*, and in that way the Qur'aan was saved from any kind of change or loss. This process was completed in the year 646 C.E., two years after 'Uthmaan became the new Caliph.

MEMORIZATION OF THE QUR'AAN

Although the total number of *Sahaabah* who had memorized all of the Qur'aan and read it back to the Prophet (ﷺ) before his death were only eight, many others memorized it after his death. In fact, with every succeeding generation of Muslims, the numbers of those who memorized all of the Qur'aan has increased. Today there are literally hundreds of thousands of Muslims throughout the world who have done so.

There is no other book, religious or otherwise, which has been memorized on this scale in recorded history. The Qur'aan is about four fifths the length of the New Testament of the Christians, yet not a single person in recorded history is known to have memorized the New Testament completely. In fact, if all of the books in the world were somehow to be destroyed, the only book which could be rewritten, word for word without a single mistake is the Glorious Qur'aan.

Significance Of The Qur'aan's Preservation

Allaah promised in the Qur'aan that He would take on the responsibility of protecting His final Word from loss. He said,

إِنَّا نَحْنُ نَزَّلْنَا الذِّكْرَ وَإِنَّا لَهُ لَحَافِظُونَ

"Verily We have revealed the Reminder (Qur'aan), and verily We shall preserve it."[1]

(Soorah al-Ḥijr (15):9)

Thus, the Qur'aan has been preserved in both the oral as well as written form the way no other religious book in history has been.

Why did Allaah preserve the Qur'aan and allow His earlier Books of Divine Revelation to be changed or lost? The answer to that question lies in the following three facts:

1. The earlier prophets and their Books were sent to particular people in particular periods of history. Once the period ended, a new prophet was sent with a new Book to replace the previous Book. So, it was not necessary that these Books be preserved by Allaah, Himself. The preservation of the earlier Books was left up to the people as a test for them. Thus, when the people went astray, they changed what was written in the books which the prophets brought, in order to make allowable the things which were forbidden to them. In that way all of the earlier Books of Revelation became either changed or lost.

2. The Prophet Muhammad (ﷺ) was the last prophet whom Allaah sent, and he was not sent to a particular people or a particular time. He was sent to all of mankind until the end of the world. Allaah said in the Qur'aan:

وَمَا أَرْسَلْنَاكَ إِلَّا كَافَّةً لِّلنَّاسِ بَشِيرًا وَنَذِيرًا وَلَكِنَّ أَكْثَرَ النَّاسِ لَا يَعْلَمُونَ

"We have only sent you (Muḥammad) as a giver of glad tidings and a warner to all mankind, but most men do not understand."

(Soorah Saba (34):28)

Thus, his Book of revelation, the Qur'aan, had to be specially preserved from any form of change or loss so that it would be available to all the generations of man until the last day of the world.

3. The Qur'aan was the main miracle which was given to Prophet Muḥammad (ﷺ) to prove that he was a true prophet of God and not an imposter. So, the Qur'aan had to be saved to prove to the later generations that Muḥammad (ﷺ) was really the last prophet of God. All of the false prophets who came after Prophet Muḥammad (ﷺ) brought books which they claimed to be revealed from Allaah, but none of them have the miraculous ability to be memorized by thousands, nor have they improved on the message in the Qur'aan.

The significance of the Qur'aan's preservation is that Islaam has been kept in its original purity because of it. Man can always return to the sources of Islaam no matter what people may have added or forgotten in time. All of the essential principles of Islaam are to be found in the Qur'aan. Consequently, the preservation of the Qur'aan meant the preservation of Islaam in its final form. The loss of the Gospel of Jesus means that Christians can never return to the true teachings of Prophet Jesus except by accepting Islaam. Similarly, the original Torah was lost when Prophet Soloman's Temple in Jerusalem was destroyed by the Babylonians. Thus, the Jews can not return to the pure teachings of Prophet Moses except by following Islaam.

It is only in Islaam that the pure teachings of the prophets have been preserved without any change. That is why Allaah said in the Qur'aan,

$$ إِنَّ ٱلدِّينَ عِندَ ٱللَّهِ ٱلْإِسْلَٰمُ $$

"Verily the only acceptable religion to Allaah is Islaam."

(Soorah Aal 'Imraan (3):19)

QUESTIONS

1. Allaah made sure that the Prophet (ﷺ) preserved the Qur'aan by
   (a) sending it on written pages with angel Jibreel.
   (b) revealing the whole Qur'aan at one time in the beginning of his prophethood.
   (c) teaching the Prophet (ﷺ) how to read and write
   (d) allowing the Prophet (ﷺ) to write down whatever Jibreel recited to him.
   (e) causing him to remember it without any effort on his part.

2. The Prophet (ﷺ) insured that the Qur'aan was not lost by
   (a) having his companions record the whole Qur'aan in one book before he died.
   (b) writing it down for his companions and leaving it with his wife Hafsah.
   (c) teaching his companions the Qur'aan and by having those who could write record it.
   (d) having angel Jibreel teach it to his companions.
   (e) giving it to Abu Bakr before he died.

3. The Qur'aan was not written down in one book during the Prophet's (ﷺ) lifetime because
   (a) the Prophet (ﷺ) forgot some of the Qur'aan.
   (b) the companions of the Prophet (ﷺ) could not read or write.
   (c) the companions were more concerned with recording and memorizing it.
   (d) the Prophet (ﷺ) forbade his companions from doing so.
   (e) many companions who memorized the Qur'aan were killed during the *Riddah* wars.

4. The Qur'aan was first recorded in one book
   (a) during the era of Caliph 'Umar, because many who had memorized the Qur'aan were dying of old age.
   (b) because the false prophet, Musaylimah, and the false

prophetess Sajaah were trying to imitate the Qur'aan during the *Riddah* wars.

(c) in Caliph Abu Bakr's time, because new Muslims were making mistakes in the recitation of the Qur'aan which led to confusion.

(d) because many Muslims who had memorized large portions of the Qur'aan were being killed during the wars of apostasy in Abu Bakr's time.

(e) in the time of Caliph 'Uthmaan, because he sent an official copy of the Qur'aan to the capitals.

5. The *Sahaabee* who was chosen to write down the whole Qur'aan in one book was
   (a) Hudhayfah ibn al-Yamaan.
   (b) Abu Bakr as-Siddeeq.
   (c) Zayd ibn Thaabit.
   (d) 'Umar ibn al-Khattaab.
   (e) 'Uthmaan ibn 'Affaan.

6. Mention four reasons why he was chosen.

7. The reason for the second writing of the Qur'aan was that
   (a) the original copy of the Qur'aan was lost.
   (b) many Muslims were being killed during the battles against the false prophets.
   (c) Caliph 'Uthmaan wanted to have his own personal copy.
   (d) new Muslims were translating the Qur'aan in their own languages.
   (e) confusion in the recitation of the Qur'aan had developed.

8. Until the second writing, the original copy of the Qur'aan was
   (a) kept with Abu Bakr, the first Caliph.
   (b) lost after the murder of the second Caliph, 'Umar ibn al-Khataab.
   (c) remained with 'Aa'eshah, daughter of Abu Bakr and wife of the Prophet (鑾).

(d) kept by 'Umar's daughter Hafṣah.

(e) stored in Zaid ibn Thaabit's house.

9. Allaah preserved the Qur'aan and allowed the earlier books of revelation to be lost

   (a) because He wanted to punish the earlier peoples for disbelieving in their Prophets.

   (b) because the earlier books were much longer than the Qur'aan.

   (c) because the earlier prophets and their books were sent to particular people and not all mankind.

   (d) because Prophet Muḥammad was an Arabian Prophet and he was sent only to the Arabs.

   (e) since Prophet Muḥammad (ﷺ) was not sent to all mankind during his lifetime.

10. Why was it important that Allaah preserve the Qur'aan?

    (a) The Qur'aan was the main miracle of Prophet Muḥammad (ﷺ), so it had to be preserved to prove to all generations that he was a true prophet.

    (b) Since Prophet Muḥammad (ﷺ) was an Arab Prophet, the Qur'aan needed to be preserved to prove to the Arabs that he was a Prophet.

    (c) The books of the Christians and Jews and the message of the earlier prophets were preserved and were competing with Islaam.

    (d) Because many of those who memorized large portions of the Qur'aan were being killed in the *Riddah* wars.

    (e) The Qur'aan is a book of revelation, thus it had to be preserved for future generations.

11. The significance of the Qur'aan's preservation is that

    (a) the gospel of Jesus was lost, thus Christians can never return to the true teachings of Jesus.

    (b) the original Torah of Prophet Moses was lost when Solomon's temple was destroyed by the Babylonians.

    (c) all false prophets who came after Prophet Muḥammad

(ﷺ) brought books which they claimed were revealed by Allaah.

(d) the pure teachings of the prophets have been preserved only in the Gospel and the Torah till today.

(e) Islaam has been kept in its original purity without any change or loss because of it.

5. TAFSEER SOORAH AL-MAA'OON (107)

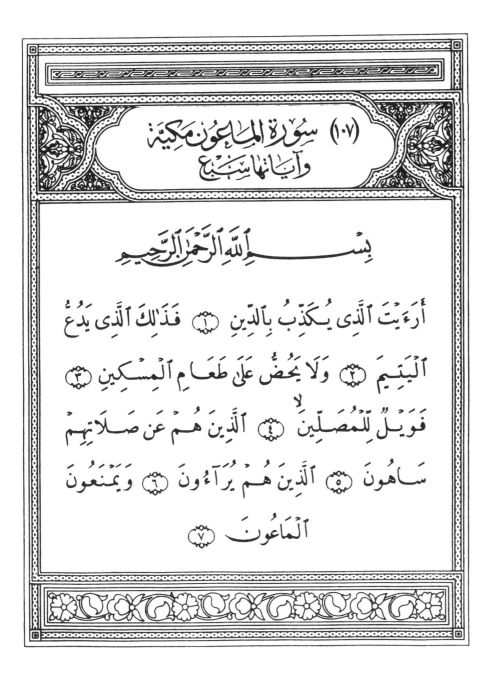

بِسْمِ اللَّهِ الرَّحْمَنِ الرَّحِيمِ

أَرَءَيْتَ الَّذِى يُكَذِّبُ بِالدِّينِ ۝ فَذَلِكَ الَّذِى يَدُعُّ الْيَتِيمَ ۝ وَلَا يَحُضُّ عَلَى طَعَامِ الْمِسْكِينِ ۝ فَوَيْلٌ لِّلْمُصَلِّينَ ۝ الَّذِينَ هُمْ عَن صَلَاتِهِمْ سَاهُونَ ۝ الَّذِينَ هُمْ يُرَآءُونَ ۝ وَيَمْنَعُونَ الْمَاعُونَ ۝

Soorah

The Qur'aan contains 114 sections which are like chapters. Allaah refers to them in the Qur'aan as *Soorahs*.

$$ وَإِن كُنتُمْ فِي رَيْبٍ مِّمَّا نَزَّلْنَا عَلَىٰ عَبْدِنَا فَأْتُوا بِسُورَةٍ مِّن مِّثْلِهِۦ $$

"If you are in doubt about what we have revealed to our servant (Muḥammad), bring one chapter (Soorah) like it."

(Soorah al-Baqarah (2):23)

Name of the Soorah

The name *Maa'oon* literally means a commonly used instrument like a bucket or a pot. However, in this *Soorah* it refers to help or kindness which everyone should be willing to share. It is the very last word which occurs in the *Soorah*. This *Soorah*, however, has a number of other names. It is called *Soorah Ara'ayta* which literally means 'have you seen'. This name was chosen because the phrase *Ara'ayta* represents the opening words of the *Soorah*. Another of its names is *Soorah ad-Deen* which literally means 'an account or explanation for one's behaviour.' This name is very suitable because the whole of the *Soorah* represents a list of the main signs by which one who disbelieves in the Day of Judgement may be recognized. The *Soorah* has also been named *Soorah al-Yateem* which literally means 'The Orphan'. The *Soorah* talks about the orphan in its opening verses.

Place of Revelation

The *Soorah* was taught to the Prophet (ﷺ) by angel Jibreel while he was in Makkah. It was revealed immediately after *Soorah at-Takaathur* (102) but the Prophet (ﷺ) later had it placed after *Soorah Quraysh* (106). The reason why the order of this and other *Soorahs* was changed is because the *Soorahs* were originally revealed to solve particular problems which the Prophet (ﷺ) and his companions were facing. Once the revelation was complete, the *Soorahs* needed rearranging for reading and recitation. Thus, the Prophet (ﷺ) was guided by Allaah to reorder the *Soorahs* as they were recorded and memorized for future generations of Muslims who would never see him, but who would believe in him and memorize Allaah's Book which he brought.

The Reason for this Revelation

Allaah teaches the Believers some very important lessons in this short *Soorah*. The main lesson is that true belief, which we call *Eemaan*, must produce good deeds. Likewise, bad deeds are to be taken as clear proof of either a very weak belief or actual disbelief, which we call *Kufr*. He also teaches us that good deeds which are not a result of true belief, will not be done properly. Since such deeds are only for show, they will never be done regularly nor in the form which is recommended. Therefore, if we find ourselves becoming lazy in our duties to Allaah, it is a sign for us to know that something is wrong with our faith. We should remember Allaah, ask His forgiveness, and begin to do our duties well.

SOORAH AL-MAA'OON

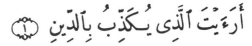

1. Have you seen the one who disbelieves in the Account?

Allaah here asks us if we have noticed the way one who does not believe in the Day of Judgement acts. Allaah is not asking this question for us to answer yes or no. He is, in fact, telling us that we should carefully observe the way such a disbeliever acts. Those people who do not feel that they will eventually have to stand before God and answer for all that they did, will act in certain ways. These ways are like signs. Whoever has them disbelieves in the Judgement, no matter how much they say they believe. The believers have to know and recognize these signs in order that they may be able to spot the enemies of Allaah and beware of them. They also have to know these signs to make sure that they are not themselves showing them, because they are the signs of *Kufr* (disbelief).

$$\text{فَذَٰلِكَ ٱلَّذِى يَدُعُّ ٱلْيَتِيمَ} \textcircled{2}$$

2. That is the one who pushes away the orphan.

The first sign of disbelief in the Day of Judgement which Allaah has chosen to mention is that of 'pushing away the orphan'. 'Pushing away the orphan' means preventing the child who has no father to look after him from receiving what belongs to him. It was the practice among the Arabs of the Prophet's (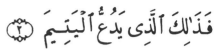) time to prevent women and children from inheriting, if their husbands or fathers died. One who does not believe that he will have to answer for all that he does in this life, is prepared to cheat even his own relatives out of their rights. If he is made a guardian over an orphan relative, he spends whatever wealth that his relative has or he simply adds it to his own personal wealth. When his orphan relative grows up, he then refuses to return the orphan's wealth. By pointing out this bad practise, Allaah is also advising us to be trustworthy. Whenever something is given to us to look after, we must make sure that we return it in the same way that we received it. Allaah emphasizes this point throughout the Qur'aan by commanding the Believers to fulfill their trusts.

$$\text{يَٰأَيُّهَا ٱلَّذِينَ ءَامَنُوٓا أَوْفُوا بِٱلْعُقُودِ}$$

"O you who believe. Fulfil (all) obligations"
(Soorah al-Maa'idah (5):1)

$$\text{وَلَا يَحُضُّ عَلَىٰ طَعَامِ ٱلْمِسْكِينِ} \textcircled{3}$$

3. Nor does he encourage the feeding of the poor.

The second major sign of disbelief in the Day of Judgement is that the disbeliever rarely ever gives charity. He is a stingy individual who holds on to his money very tightly. If he spends his wealth, he does so only on himself and on his family. He feels that his wealth is a result of his own hard work, and that the poor have no money because of their laziness.

But, if he were to look around honestly, he would see many who have worked harder than himself and have much less than him. Likewise, he would also see others who have made much less effort than himself, yet they have more than him. In fact, if wealth and success were the direct result of hard work, the poor people of this world, who work all day, would be the richest. Wealth is really only a blessing from Allaah which He uses to test mankind. The question on the test is: Will man be thankful to Allaah and prove it by sharing it with others, or will he be ungrateful and prove it by being stingy?

In this verse, Allaah teaches the true Believer to be generous and give charity regularly. Islaam has made charity an obligation on those who have more than their basic needs. *Zakaah* is the tax system in Islaam which takes wealth from the well-to-do and distributes it among the poor. This system not only protects the weaker members of society, but it also trains the stronger members to share their blessings with others. It is a part of man's nature to want to hold on to what is his, so he has to be taught to share.

فَوَيْلٌ لِّلْمُصَلِّينَ ﴿٤﴾

4. So, woe to those who pray,

Woe means bad wishes. But why would Allaah make bad wishes on people who pray. Especially when it was He who made *Salaah* (prayer) a must for Muslims, five times per day.

فَأَقِيمُوا الصَّلَوٰةَ إِنَّ الصَّلَوٰةَ كَانَتْ عَلَى الْمُؤْمِنِينَ كِتَابًا مَّوْقُوتًا

"Set up regular prayers because prayers are compulsory for believers at set times."

(Soorah an-Nisaa' (4):103)

The Prophet (ﷺ) also said that Islaam is built on five pillars, the second of which is making regular prayers. Therefore, this verse can not be properly understood by itself, as its meaning would then be against the basic teachings of the Qur'aan and Islaam. We have to look at the following verse in order to find out just exactly what Allaah means here.

$$\text{ٱلَّذِينَ هُمْ عَن صَلَاتِهِمْ سَاهُونَ ۝}$$

5. Those who are careless about their Prayers (Salaah),

Now the meaning becomes clear. Allaah is not saying woe to all those who make *Salaah*. The woe is only on some people who make *Salaah*. Bad wishes are on those who only pretend to pray. Those go through all the motions of prayer, but in a careless manner. Such careless people often start the *Salaah* late, or, when they are praying alone, they delay the *Salaah* and pray it out of its time. They often do the *Salaah* quickly and without any concentration. They look around or at their watches and even find reason to laugh during the *Salaah*. Such are the people who will be punished even though they made their required prayers.

Salaah, in its proper form, is the first thing which Allaah has made compulsory on those who have declared their belief in Him. It is, therefore, proof of one's belief in Allaah. That is why the careless *Salaah* becomes a sign of a man's disbelief in the Judgement. The one who prays carelessly can not possibly believe that Allaah is watching him, nor can he believe that he will be asked about how he made his *Salaah.*

Thus, by wishing ill on those who pray carelessly, Allaah is advising the believers to be careful with their prayers. Elsewhere in the Qur'aan Allaah encourages care in prayers by describing the true believers as follows:

$$\text{وَٱلَّذِينَ هُمْ عَلَىٰ صَلَوَٰتِهِمْ يُحَافِظُونَ}$$

"And those who guard their prayers."

(Soorah al-Mu'minoon (23):9)

Once when the Prophet (ﷺ) was asked, "Which deed is the best?"

He replied, *"Prayer on time."*[1] On another occasion he said, *"If you are praying, you should not look around, for certainly (looking around) is booty which Satan steals from Allaah's servant's prayer."*[2]

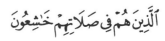

6. Those who only want to be seen.

In this verse Allaah explains the main intention of those who pray carelessly. They do so in order that others may see them. They are not praying to please Allaah, since they do not really believe in Him. They make *Salaah* to make people think that they are Muslims. Because of their fear that, if someone sees them not praying they may be punished or scolded, they pretend to pray. At schools where *Salaah* is held, some students pray because they are afraid that one of the teachers or the principal will punish them. At home, some children pray because their parents have threatened to beat them if they do not pray. Those who pray for such reasons do not really know who Allaah is, even though they may have Muslim names and their parents may really be Muslims. Islaam is not something which can be inherited from one's parents like wealth or nationality. True Islaam has to be chosen by each and every individual. Allaah mentions this bad intention to advise the believers to be sincere in their prayers. In another verse Allaah describes the true believers as:

الَّذِينَ هُمْ فِى صَلَاتِهِمْ خَشِعُونَ

"Those who humble themselves in their prayers."

(Soorah al-Mu'minoon (23):2)

---

[1] Collected by al-Bukhaaree *(Sahih Al-Bukhari* (Arabic-English), vol. 1, p. 300, no. 505) and Muslim).

[2] Collected by al-Bukhaaree *(Sahih Al-Bukhari* (Arabic-English), vol. 1, p. 401, no. 718) and at-Tirmidhee.

The Prophet Muhammad (ﷺ) was reported to have said, "*Pray (each prayer) like a farewell prayer.*"[1] We should pray every *Salaah* as if it were our last. He also strongly warned us by calling the act of praying to be seen *"Hidden Shirk"*.

$$\text{وَيَمْنَعُونَ ٱلْمَاعُونَ} \quad \text{(٧)}$$

7. And they refuse to give help.

The proof that those who are careless in their *Salaah* only pray to be seen is that they are unwilling to do even the simplest acts of kindness. If their neighbours ask to borrow commonly used instruments, like a bucket or a pot, they find some excuse to not lend them. *Salaah* which is done because of a true belief in Allaah prevents the one who makes it from extreme levels of unkindness such as this. How can one say, *"al-Hamdu lillaah* (i.e. all thanks and praise belongs to Allaah alone)" at least seventeen times every day and yet refuse to be kind. They thank Allaah for His countless kindnesses and seek His favors, yet they prefer to be unkind and mean. That does not make sense at all. Allaah says that prayer should stop the believers from bad deeds,

$$\text{إِنَّ ٱلصَّلَوٰةَ تَنْهَىٰ عَنِ ٱلْفَحْشَآءِ وَٱلْمُنكَرِ}$$

"Surely prayer *(Salaah)* prevents evil speech and evil deeds.."

(Soorah al-'Ankaboot (29):45)

The only way that their unkindness can be understood is if they do not believe in what they are saying in their prayers. They are only repeating words which they memorized like parrots. Because of that, their prayers have no effect on their lives at all. They do not worship Allaah when they make *Salaah*, because they do not really believe in Him.

---

[1] Collected by Ibn Maajah and Ahmad and rated *Saheeh* by al-Albaanee in *Sifah Salaah an-Nabee*, p. 63.

Summary

By pointing out to the Believers some of the major signs of disbelief, Allaah in fact warns them to avoid these signs. He encourages them to develop the signs of righteousness and true belief which are the opposite of these signs. The true Believer is trustworthy, generous and kind. He is also very careful about his *Salaah*, because it is his main link with Allaah. His firm belief in the Judgement causes him to do good deeds whenever he can. No good deed is unimportant to him no matter how small or simple it might seem.

QUESTIONS

1. The word *Maa'oon* in Soorah al-Maa'oon means
    (a) depriving an orphan or widow of what is rightfully theirs.
    (b) praying to be seen by others instead of praying to Allaah.
    (c) carelessness in making *Salaah*.
    (d) help or kindness which everyone should be willing to give.
    (e) the unwillingness to give charity to the poor and needy.

2. Briefly explain why the order of the Soorahs was changed by the Prophet ( ) from the order in which they were revealed.

3. (a) Mention the three lessons which Allaah teaches us in *Soorah al-Maa'oon*.

    (b) Explain briefly why Allaah gives these lessons.

Verse 1. **"Have you seen the one who disbelieves in the account?"**

4. In this verse "the account" refers to
    (a) Allaah, the Creator of the universe and its contents.
    (b) the Hellfire and its torments.
    (c) the message of Islaam brought by the Prophets.
    (d) the angels who take the spirits of those who die.
    (e) the Day of Judgement.

5. Verse 2. **"That is the one who pushes away the orphan."**

    (a) Briefly explain what is meant by pushing away the orphan.

    (b) Identify the principle of disbelief about which this verse speaks.

    (c) Mention the quality which Allaah wishes the Believers to develop in the above mentioned verse.

Verse 3. **"Nor does he encourage the feeding of the poor."**

6. Mention briefly the second major sign of disbelief in the Day of Judgement found in this verse.

7. The stingy individual considers his wealth to be

(a) a gift from God which he must share with others.
(b) a product of his efforts which no one else has any right to.
(c) a result of his own hard work which should be shared with others.
(d) a blessing from Allaah and poverty is due to laziness.
(e) a test from God so is poverty.

8. The true nature and significance of wealth is that it is
   (a) the result of hard work but it should be shared.
   (b) a blessing from God and a test of man's gratitude.
   (c) a blessing from Allaah for His righteous servants.
   (d) a test from Allaah for the disbelievers.
   (e) none of the above.

9. The characteristic of faith encouraged in verse 3 is
   (a) stinginess and hoarding of wealth.
   (b) giving regular charity only to one's family.
   (c) generosity and caring for the unfortunate.
   (d) kindness to loved ones.
   (e) sharing the wealth of others.

Verse 4 **"So woe to those who pray."**

10. The word "woe" in this verse
    (a) means stop.
    (b) refers to success for those who turn in prayer to God.
    (c) can only be understood when this verse is read along with the verse which comes after it.
    (d) means that Satan is against those who pray.
    (e) means bad wishes.

11. "Woe" is said for all those who pray
    (a) because Satan wants them to go astray.
    (b) carefully because their *Salaah* is never delayed.
    (c) on time and with complete concentration because their careful *Salaah* is a sign of true belief in the Day of Judgement.
    (d) because they cheat orphans and are stingy with their wealth.

(e) carelessly and to be seen by other people.

12. Explain why carelessness in *Salaah* is a sign of disbelief in the Day of Judgement.

13. How can people say *"al-Hamdu lillaah"* at least 17 times per day in *Salaah* and yet refuse to be kind.

14. List five signs of the disbeliever in the Judgement mentioned in this *Soorah* and the corresponding five characteristics of the true believer.

6. TAFSEER SOORAH AN-NAṢR (110)

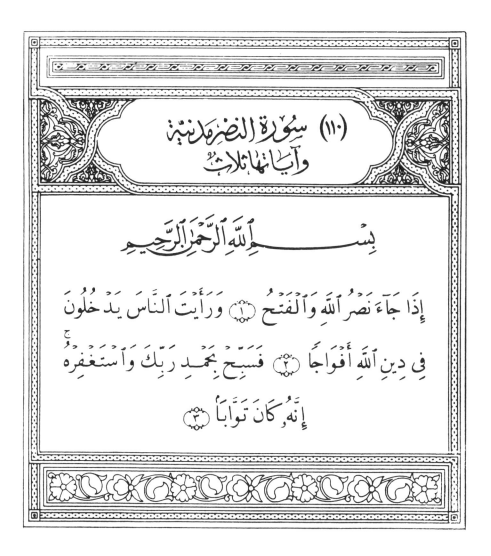

(١١٠) سُورَةُ النَّصْرِ مَدَنِيَّةٌ
وَآيَاتُهَا ثَلَاثٌ

بِسْمِ ٱللَّهِ ٱلرَّحْمَٰنِ ٱلرَّحِيمِ

إِذَا جَاءَ نَصْرُ ٱللَّهِ وَٱلْفَتْحُ ۝ وَرَأَيْتَ ٱلنَّاسَ يَدْخُلُونَ
فِى دِينِ ٱللَّهِ أَفْوَاجًا ۝ فَسَبِّحْ بِحَمْدِ رَبِّكَ وَٱسْتَغْفِرْهُ
إِنَّهُ كَانَ تَوَّابًا ۝

Name of the Soorah

The name *Naṣr* literally means 'help or aid' and it is taken from the first line of the *Soorah*. This name is very suitable for the *Soorah* because it expresses the main thought of the *Soorah* which is the coming of Allaah's help. However, this *Soorah* has also been titled *Soorah at-Tawdee‘* which means 'the farewell chapter', because it was revealed shortly before the death of the Prophet Muḥammad (ﷺ).

Place of Revelation

This *Soorah* was the last *Soorah* of the Qur'aan to be revealed and it was originally preceded by *Soorah* at-Tawbah which is now the ninth *Soorah*. The *Sahaabee* Ibn 'Umar reported that this *Soorah* was revealed in Mina during the last three days of the Prophet's (ﷺ) farewell *Hajj (Hijjah al-Widaa‘)*.

Reason for Revelation

The *Sahaabee,* Ibn 'Abbaas reported that when this *Soorah* was revealed, the Prophet (ﷺ) said, *"My death has been announced to me. that (my soul) will be taken during this (coming) year."*[1] Thus, the immediate purpose of this *Soorah* was to inform the Prophet (ﷺ) that his end was near, giving him ample time to prepare for his death. His preparations consisted of giving away his few remaining possessions, warning his followers of the greatest dangers which they will face and seeking forgiveness from Allaah for whatever errors he might have made unintentionally. However, the general reason for the revelation of this Soorah is to remind the believers not to forget Allaah and their duties to Him if He grants them success. This reminder is necessary because people tend to only remember God in times of difficulty. Instead, the believers are encouraged to praise God and thank Him for His favors, whenever they are blessed with success. In fact, to do so is one of the signs of true belief according to Prophet

---

[1] Collected by Aḥmad and rated *Saheeh* by Aḥmad Shaakir in *al-Musnad*, vol. 3, p. 265, no. 1873.

Muhammad (ﷺ), who was reported to have said, *"The affair of the believer is amazing, for all his situations are beneficial for him, and this is only in the case of the believer. If good times come to him he is thankful, and thus it was good for him; and if bad times befall him he is patient, and it is also good for him."* [1]

The believers are also advised to remember to ask Allaah's forgiveness for their sins, because no one is free from sin, and it is only Allaah who can forgive the sins of men. If one does not seek forgiveness, he will become a truly evil individual destined for Hell.

Hadeeth Concerning This Soorah

The *Sahaabee,* Ibn 'Abbaas, said, " 'Umar ibn al-Khattaab (the second Caliph) used to invite me to gatherings with older *Sahaabah*, who had taken part in the battle of Badr along with the Prophet (ﷺ). However, some of them were bothered by my presence and said, 'Why does he include this little boy along with us when we all have sons just like him (whom we have left at home)?' When 'Umar detected their dissatisfaction, he said, 'You all do not really know who he is.' One day he called all of them together and included me among them. He then said, 'What do you all say concerning Allaah's statement, *Edhaa jaa'a Nasrullaahi wal-Fat-h?'* Some of them said, 'Allaah orders us to praise Him and ask His forgiveness if He helps us and gives us victory.' However, some of them remained silent not saying anything. 'Umar turned to me and asked me my opinion, and I replied that it was not as they said. He then asked me to explain. So, I said, 'It was the end of Allaah's messenger (the end of his life) that Allaah was informing him of. Allaah said, **When Allaah's help and victory comes,** that is a sign of your end, **so glorify and praise your Lord, seeking His forgiveness because He is most forgiving.'** 'Umar added that he

---

[1] Reported by Suhayb and collected by Muslim *(Sahih Muslim* (English Trans.), vol. 4, p. 1541, no. 7138).

did not know of any other explanation or interpretation than the one which I made."[1]

In this incident, 'Umar showed the elder *Sahaabah* that inspite of Ibn 'Abbaas' young age, he was more knowledgeable about the Qur'aan than they were. Therefore, he deserved to be among them on the Council. Though Islaam teaches respect of elders, it teaches a greater respect for knowledge. The Prophet (ﷺ) taught that formal prayers *(Salaah)* were to be led by the one who memorized the most Qur'aan. 'Amr ibn Salamah reported that his father once said, *"I've come to you all from the true Prophet (ﷺ) who said, 'When the time for Salaah comes, one of you should make the Adhaan and the one with the most Qur'aan (memorized) should lead you.'* 'Amr went on to say, *"They looked around and found no one knowing more Qur'aan than me, so they put me forward (to lead the prayer) and I was only six or seven years old at that time."*[2]

SOORAH AN-NAṢR

إِذَا جَآءَ نَصْرُ ٱللَّهِ وَٱلْفَتْحُ ﴿١﴾

1. When the help and victory of Allaah comes

Allaah begins this *Soorah* by recounting to the Prophet (ﷺ) the great blessings which He had given him. The first being victory over all of his enemies. The Qurayshite tribe which ruled Makkah and which had driven the Prophet (ﷺ) and his early companions out of their homes ten years earlier were themselves thoroughly crushed in

---

[1] Collected by al-Bukhaaree *(Sahih Al-Bukhari* (Arabic-English), vol. 6, pp. 465-6, no. 494).

[2] Collected by al-Bukhaaree *(Sahih Al-Bukhari* (Arabic-English), vol. 5, pp. 413-4, no. 595), Abu Daawood *(Sunan Abu Dawud* (English Trans.), vol. 1, p. 154, no. 485) and an-Nasaa'ee.

the eighth year after the *Hijrah*. The Makkans surrendered without a fight and the Prophet (ﷺ) marched straight to the Ka'bah and destroyed all of the idols and sacrificial altars in and around the Ka'bah. The Prophet (ﷺ) and his followers' conquest of Makkah is referred to in this verse as the "Victory of Allaah" in order to emphasize to the Prophet (ﷺ) and the believers that success is from Allaah. Prophets before Muhammad (ﷺ) all preached the message of Islaam and tried to establish it among their people; however, many of them were not given success by Allaah. Some like Prophet Yahyaa, were killed, or tortured by their people, and others, like Prophet Ibraheem, were driven out of their homeland. Since the message of Islaam as brought by Prophet Muhammad (ﷺ) was to be the final one, Allaah gave the last Prophet (ﷺ) victory to establish the religion of Islaam in Arabia as a basis for spreading it in its pure form throughout the world. This help from Allaah was very important, because even though the message of Prophet 'Eesaa (Jesus) was spread after Allaah lifted him up, it did not remain in its original form.

وَرَأَيْتَ ٱلنَّاسَ يَدْخُلُونَ فِى دِينِ ٱللَّهِ أَفْوَاجًا ﴿٢﴾

2. And you see droves of people entering Allaah's religion

The second blessing which Allaah gave the Prophet (ﷺ) was that the majority of the people with whom he had direct contact all accepted Islaam. After the fall of Makkah, huge numbers of people came into Islaam. During the Prophet's thirteen years of preaching Islaam in Makkah, a little more than three hundred people embraced Islaam. However, after his emigration to Madeenah, many more people began to accept Islaam. And, following the Prophet's conquest of Makkah, whole families and tribes began to enter Islaam at one time. In fact, the year after the victory over the Makkans is recorded in history as the *"Year of the Delegations"*, because of the large number of ambassadors sent by tribes from all corners of the

Arabian peninsula. These delegations came to the Prophet (ﷺ) in Madeenah and accepted Islaam on behalf of their clans or tribes. Before they returned to their tribes, the Prophet (ﷺ) would assign to each delegation one of his *Sahaabah*, who knew Islaam well enough to teach them.

Many of the early prophets were rejected by their people, so the wide acceptance of Islaam was truly a great blessing for the Prophet Muhammad (ﷺ). The spread of Islaam at such an early stage was necessary, since this was the final message of Islaam for all mankind. And, the more people who heard it and lived it during the Prophet's (ﷺ) lifetime, the better it would be preserved for all times.

$$فَسَبِّحْ بِحَمْدِ رَبِّكَ وَاسْتَغْفِرْهُ$$

3. Glorify and praise your Lord and ask His forgiveness

In this verse Allaah explains what He wants the Prophet (ﷺ) to do after he has observed the successes of victory and the nation-wide acceptance of Islaam. First, the Prophet (ﷺ) was told to give thanks to his Lord for the success which He had given him by glorifying and praising Him. Because, success was not a direct result of his own efforts. And, secondly, since these successes represent the completion of the prophethood and its message, the Prophet (ﷺ) should now prepare to leave this world by seeking God's forgiveness. Forgiveness for his unintentional errors in judging between the good and the better. This did not include intentional sins, because the Prophet (ﷺ) was *Ma'soom*, free from such errors. For example, on one occasion a blind Muslim, Ibn Umm Maktoom approached the Prophet (ﷺ) just as he was about to explain Islaam to a gathering of leaders from the Qurayshite tribe, and the Prophet (ﷺ) frowned and ignored him. The Prophet (ﷺ) did not want to lose this golden opportunity to call the Qurayshite leaders to Islaam, because their acceptance would mean the acceptance of the rest of the tribe. So he avoided Ibn Umm Maktoom, since he was already Muslim and could be taught later. However, Allaah revealed in *Soorah 'Abasa* that the Prophet's decision was wrong. The one who had come seeking knowledge of Islaam should have been given preference over non-Muslims whom he had to call, no matter how important they might have been. In fact, when the Prophet (ﷺ) sat with the Qurayshite leaders and explained Islaam to them, they agreed to follow him on condition that he get rid of all his "low-class" Muslim followers, as they could not accept former slaves and poor people as their equals. The Prophet (ﷺ) had to reject their condition, as it was opposed to the Islamic principle of brotherhood of the believers. These same leaders eventually became the greatest enemies of Islaam, spilled the blood of many Muslims, and most died or were killed without ever accepting Islaam.

Another example can be found in the case of prisoners of the Battle of Badr. After the first battle between the Muslims and the pagan Makkans, the Prophet (ﷺ) asked the opinion of his companions about what should be done with the pagan prisoners-of-war. Abu Bakr suggested releasing them and 'Umar ibn al-Khattaab suggested that they should all be killed. The Prophet (ﷺ) chose Abu Bakr's opinion and freed them for a ransom of 400 dirhams per person and Allaah revealed the verse:

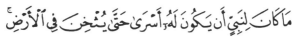

"A Prophet should not take prisoners until he has throughly conquered the land."

(Soorah al-Anfaal (8):67)[1]

The prisoners should have been killed for the many Muslims they killed and tortured in Makkah since this was the first battle against them. As a result the prisoners who were set free came and killed more Muslims in the Battle of Uhud and later battles. There were a few other errors of judgement like these which the Prophet (ﷺ) made, but

---

[1] Collected by Abu Daawood *(Sunan Abu Dawud* (English Trans.), vol. 2, p. 746, no. 2684 & 2685), and authenticated by al-Albaanee in *Saheeh Sunan Abee Daawood,* (English Trans.), vol. 2, p. 512, no. 2339 and 2340.

Allaah corrected all of them by revealing verses of the Qur'aan.

The Prophet's third wife, 'Aa'eshah, noted that Allaah's messenger (ﷺ) interpreted this verse of the Qur'aan by frequently repeating in the *Rukoo's* (bowings) and *Sujoods* (prostrations) of his prayers the phrase:

سُبْحَانَكَ اللّهُمَّ وَبِحَمْدِكَ اللّهُمَّ اغْفِرْ لِى

Subhaanak Allaahumma wa bihamdik Allaahummagh-firlee (Glory and praise be to You O Allaah. O Allaah forgive me) [1]

The Prophet (ﷺ) was also told to seek forgiveness for the sins of his followers, as an example to his followers to seek forgiveness for their sins. In other religions such as Catholicism among the Christians, the followers are told to confess their sins to priests who are supposed to be able to ask God's forgiveness for them. Most other Christians direct their prayers for forgiveness to Jesus whom they believe died on the cross to pay for the sins of all mankind. Jews on the other hand, consider themselves the chosen children of God who will inherit paradise no matter what they do; hence there is no need for seeking forgiveness. In Islaam the believers are told to seek forgiveness for their sins from Allaah alone, for none can forgive them besides Him. The Prophet Muhammad (ﷺ) taught Abu Bakr the following *Du'aa* to be said at the end of his *Salaah* just before *Tasleem:* [2]

اللّهُمَّ إِنِّى ظَلَمْتُ نَفْسِى ظُلْماً كَثِيراً وَلاَ يَغْفِرُ الذُّنُوبَ إِلاَّ أَنْتَ فَاغْفِرْ لِى مَغْفِرَةً مِنْ عِنْدِكَ وَارْحَمْنِىْ إِنَّكَ أَنْتَ الْغَفُورُ الرَّحِيْمُ

Allaahumma innee dHalamtu nafsee dHulman Katheeraa
"O Allah, verily I have really wronged myself a lot

---

[1] Collected by al-Bukhaaree, (*Sahih Al-Bukhari* (Arabic-English), vol. 6, p. 464, no. 492), Muslim, (*Sahih Muslim* (English Trans.), vol. 1, pp. 254-5, no. 981), Abu Daawood, (*Sunan Abu Dawud* (English Trans.), vol. 1, p. 224, no. 876), an-Nasaa'ee, and Ibn Maajah.

[2] Saying "*Salaam 'Alaykum wa raḥmatullaah* to complete the *Salaah*.

Wa laa yaghfirudh-dhunooba illaa ant
And none can forgive sins except You
Faghfir lee maghfiratan min 'indika war ḥamnee
So forgive me with Your forgiveness and have mercy on me
Innaka antal-Ghafoorur-Raheem
Verily you are the Most Forgiving, the Most Merciful.''[1]

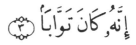

4. Surely, He is the Oft Forgiving

In the closing verse of this *Soorah*, Allaah explains the major reason for commanding the Prophet (ﷺ) and the believers to seek His forgiveness. Allaah's forgiveness in this life for those who sincerely repent and ask His forgiveness knows no bounds. He will forgive a sinner over and over again, as long as his repentance is sincerely from his heart. As for one who merely says words of repentance, but in his heart he does not feel real sorrow, there is no forgiveness for him, as the Prophet (ﷺ) said, *"Deeds are judged by their intentions."*[2] Thus, a believer should never feel that his or her sins are too great to be forgiven. Such a negative thought is from the devil, who wants man to lose hope in Allaah and thereby become a habitual sinner, a truly lost soul. It is a part of man's nature to make mistakes, or as the Prophet (ﷺ) said, *"All of Aadam's descendants habitually err, but the best of them are the habitually repentant."*[3] That is, those who constantly seek Allaah's forgiveness whenever they sin, are the best of mankind.

---

[1] Collected by al-Bukhaaree *(Sahih Al-Bukhari* (Arabic-English), vol. 8, p. 227-8, no. 338) and Muslim *(Sahih Muslim* (English Trans.), vol. 4, pp. 1419-20, no. 6533).

[2] Collected by al-Bukhaaree *(Sahih Al-Bukhari* (Arabic-English), vol. 1, p. 1, no.1).

[3] Reported by Anas ibn Maalik and collected by at-Tirmidhee, Ibn Maajah, ad-Daarimee and Ahmad and rated authentic *(Ḥasan)* by al-Arna'oot in *Jaami' al-Uṣool*, vol. 2, p. 515, no. 988.

QUESTIONS

1. (a) Mention the literal meaning of *Nasr* and its significance in the *Soorah*.

   (b) What is *Soorah an-Nasr's* other name, its literal meaning and its significance.

2. Where and when was this *Soorah* revealed?

   (a) in Makkah three days before the conquest of Madeenah.
   (b) in Minaa during the last three days of the Prophet's (ﷺ) Hajj.
   (c) in 'Arafaat three days after the Prophet's (ﷺ) farewell 'Umrah.
   (d) in Minaa three days after the conquest of Makkah.
   (e) in Madeenah, three days before the Prophet (ﷺ) began his farewell Hajj.

3. The reason for Soorah an-Nasr's revelation was
   (a) to warn the disbelievers that they will be defeated.
   (b) to inform the Prophet (ﷺ) that he should not take prisoners after the Battle of Badr.
   (c) for the *Mahr* (dowry) of one of the Prophet's (ﷺ) companions.
   (d) to inform the Prophet (ﷺ) that his death was near.
   (e) to show Ibn 'Abbaas that 'Umar ibn al-Khattaab needed him in his meetings with the elder *Sahaabah*

4. What lesson did 'Umar teach the older *Sahaabah* about Ibn 'Abbaas?

Verse 7. "When the Help and Victory of Allaah comes."

5. What is the victory mentioned in the first verse?
   (a) the defeat of the Makkans in the battle of Uhud.
   (b) the successful Hajj of the Prophet (ﷺ).

(c) the conquest of Makkah without a fight.

(d) the escape of the Prophet (ﷺ) from Madeenah to Makkah.

6. Allaah refers to this victory as Allaah's victory.

(a) to emphasize to the Prophet (ﷺ) and the believers that victory was soon to come.

(b) because Allaah caused many people to enter Islaam.

(c) to inform the Prophet (ﷺ) and the believers that they do not need to fight because victory is from Allaah.

(d) because defeat and failure is from Satan.

(e) to remind the Prophet (ﷺ) and the believers that success comes only from Allaah.

7. (a) Describe the great event which followed the help and victory of Allaah.

(b) What was "*The Year of Delegations*" and why was it called that?

8. Why should the Prophet (ﷺ) praise and glorify Allaah?

9. Why should he ask forgiveness when he was free from error "*Ma'soom*"?

10. An example of the Prophet's errors may be seen in his

(a) turning away from the Qurayshite chiefs in order to teach a blind Muslim.

(b) conquest of Makkah without fighting the Makkans.

(c) execution of the prisoners of war after the Battle of Badr.

(d) avoiding a blind Muslim's request in order to explain Islaam to the Qurayshite chiefs.

(e) freeing all the prisoners after the Battle of Uhud.

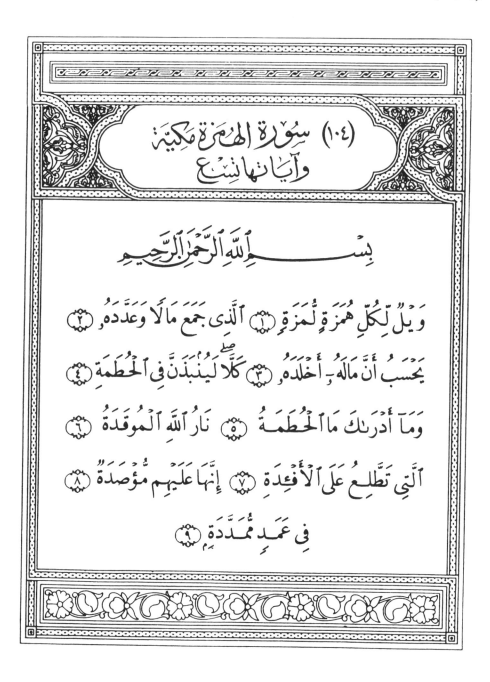

Name of the Soorah

The name *Humazah* literally means 'the slanderer or one who tells lies about people.' It is the last word of the first verse. It is also a good title for the *Soorah,* since the whole *Soorah* is a description of the slanderer's traits and the punishment which awaits him in the next life.

Place of Revelation

This Soorah was also revealed to the Prophet (ﷺ) at the beginning of his mission in Makkah. It came immediately after Soorah al-Qiyaamah (75) but the Prophet (ﷺ) later placed it after Soorah al-'Asr (103).

The Reason for This Revelation

In the early days of the Prophethood, the tribe of Quraysh used to make fun of the Prophet (ﷺ) and his followers. They also used to make up bad stories about the Prophet (ﷺ). For example, they used to say that he was bewitched or mad and they would make up jokes about him. They also used to claim that he had a *Jinn* who used to teach him the Qur'aan. Or, they would say that the Qur'aan was a magical spell.

This is the way of the disbelievers even today. They like to make fun of the Believers and they often tell lies about Islaam and its followers. The way Muslim women dress is funny to them and they claim that Islaam is unfair to women because it does not allow them to walk around half-naked as many women do in some non-Muslim lands.

Thus, Allaah revealed this *Soorah* to point out the traits of the disbelievers in order that the Believers may avoid them. He also wanted to let them know about the punishment prepared for those who make fun of Islaam and its true followers. Allaah describes the punishment in detail to scare the disbelievers who have some doubts and to reassure the Believers that their choice of Islaam over *Kufr* was right.

SOORAH AL-HUMAZAH

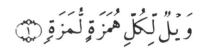

1. Woe be on every slandering backbiter,

Allaah, Most Great and Glorious, sends bad wishes to all who tell lies about innocent people. Those who do that are usually backbiters, because they do so behind people's backs and not to their faces. Allaah's bad wishes is like a curse on them which causes misfortune to happen to them in this life and the next.

Islaam is firmly against slander and backbiting in all its forms. Abu Hurayrah reported that on one occasion the Prophet (ﷺ) asked the companions, *"Do you know what backbiting (Gheebah) is?"* They replied, *"Allaah and His Messenger (ﷺ) know best."* He said, *"It is mentioning something about your brother that he does not like."* Someone asked, *"What if what I say about my brother is true?"* The Prophet (ﷺ) replied, *"If what you said about him is true you have backbitten and if it was not true you have slandered."*[1] One who is caught slandering women by accusing them of having unlawful relations with men is punished with eighty lashes. In another verse of the Qur'aan Allaah says:

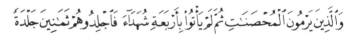

"And those who accuse chaste women without bringing four witnesses should be flogged eighty times..."

(Soorah an-Noor (24):4)

And, Allaah has compared backbiting with eating one's brother's flesh after he has died.

---

[1] Collected by Muslim *(Sahih Muslim* (English Trans.), vol. 4, p. 1369, no. 6265).

"And do not backbite each other. Would any of you like to eat the flesh of his dead brother? You would dislike it."

(Soorah al-Ḥujuraat (49):12)

Allaah made this comparison to show us how terrible backbiting is. The believer should hate backbiting the way he would hate to eat his dead brother's flesh. Thus, even the listening to slander or backbiting without opposing it is considered a sin.

Perhaps the most serious form of slander is that of those who slander Allaah. Some say that Allaah has a son and others say He is the third of three gods. But the worst are those who say that Allaah does not really exist. God, to them, is only a superstition which ancient people made up in order to explain things which they did not understand. Thus, according to them, religion is simply a hoax and the Prophets were all phonies. They lie about Allaah, His Prophets, His Books and His Religion.[1]

$$ٱلَّذِى جَمَعَ مَالًا وَعَدَّدَهُ ۝$$

2. Who gathered wealth and counted it.

Because Allaah and religion has no meaning to the slanderer, life becomes a meaningless animal existence. According to him there is no purpose to life, so the most important thing is to have a good time. To have a good time one must have a lot of wealth. Thus, the slanderer spends most of his time trying to gather all the wealth that he can and in any way that he can. A lot of his time is also spent adding it up in order to make sure none is lost and to be certain that it is always increasing.

---

[1] This was the most serious form of slander because it denied the reason for our creation. Allaah created man to worship him, therefore, to disbelieve in Him and say he is unreal is the greatest crime that man may commit. This is why Allaah said that He would forgive all sins except *Shirk*. In the Qur'aan Allaah says: **"Verily Allaah does not forgive making *Shirk*, but He forgives anything less than that for whom He pleases."** (Soorah an-Nisaa' (4):84 and 116).

This blind individual loves to make fun of others who are less fortunate than himself. And, he considers himself to be better than them. The fact that his wealth is only a part of a test which Allaah has given him does not even cross his mind. As far as he is concerned, his wealth is simply the result of his hard work or his good luck. If he gives away any of his wealth to anyone outside of his family, it is done to buy friends or control enemies. He would never think to give in charity because he has more than he needs, for that would only decrease his wealth.

$$يَحْسَبُ أَنَّ مَالَهُ أَخْلَدَهُ ۝$$

3. He thinks that his wealth has made him immortal.

The one who slanders God becomes so wrapped-up in the pleasures of this life that he begins to wish that he will not have to die. He starts to think that his great wealth should be able to keep him alive forever. Consequently, the rich donate countless millions of dollars to scientific research on finding a cure for old-age. They actually believe that man will eventually find a cure for death. Some wealthy people have paid huge amounts of money to have their bodies frozen when they die. Their bodies are then put in refrigerated metal coffins in the hope that when man eventually discovers the cure for death, their bodies will be thawed out and brought back to life! The ancient Egyptians also had a similar belief. The Pharaohs and the rich had their dead bodies preserved and buried with their riches in the belief that they would later come back to life. But, their graves have now been robbed and their bodies have been put on display in countless museums around the world. Allaah's Messenger (ﷺ) told his companions that there is no cure for old-age. Usaamah ibn Shurayk reported that Prophet Muhammad (ﷺ) said, *"Servants of Allaah, treat each other's sicknesses. For surely Allaah, Glory be to Him, has not sent down a disease along with a cure except old age."*[1] Because of that

---

[1] Collected by at-Tirmidhee, Abu Daawood *(Sunan Abu Dawud* (English Trans.), vol. 3, p. 1083, no. 3846), Ibn Maajah and Ahmad, and rated *Saheeh* in *Saheeh Sunan Abee Daawood*, vol. 2, p. 731, no. 3264.

Muslims would never waste any time or effort in trying to cure death. Satan tricked Aadam into disobeying God by promising him eternal life. Allaah informed us about this incident so that we would not be led astray in this way. Allaah said in the Qur'aan:

فَوَسْوَسَ لَهُمَا ٱلشَّيْطَٰنُ لِيُبْدِىَ لَهُمَا مَا وُۥرِىَ عَنْهُمَا مِن سَوْءَٰتِهِمَا وَقَالَ مَا نَهَىٰكُمَا رَبُّكُمَا عَنْ هَٰذِهِ ٱلشَّجَرَةِ إِلَّآ أَن تَكُونَا مَلَكَيْنِ أَوْ تَكُونَا مِنَ ٱلْخَٰلِدِينَ

"Then Satan began to whisper to them…saying, 'Your Lord only forbade you this tree so that you do not become angels or of those who live forever.' "

(Soorah al-A'raaf (7):20)

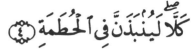

4. No; but surely he will be thrown into *al-Ḥuṭamah*.

Allaah tells this foolish individual no, he will not live forever. Every living thing must die and nothing comes back to life in this world. That is the law which Allaah has set and no living being can break it. In another chapter of the Qur'aan Allaah says:

كُلُّ نَفْسٍ ذَآئِقَةُ ٱلْمَوْتِ

"Every soul will taste death.."

(Soorah Aal 'Imraan (3):185)

وَمِن وَرَآئِهِم بَرْزَخٌ إِلَىٰ يَوْمِ يُبْعَثُونَ

"Behind them is a partition *(Barzakh)* until the day they are resurrected."

(Soorah al-Mu'minoon (23):100)

Instead of coming back to life and enjoying some more good times on the earth, he will be cast into a creature called *al-Ḥuṭamah*. The name *al-Ḥuṭamah* means the crusher, something which smashes into pieces whatever is put into it. There will be no pleasure for him as his body and soul is completely destroyed. All that he will experience after his death is pain upon pain.

$$\text{وَمَآ أَدْرَىٰكَ مَا ٱلْحُطَمَةُ ﴿٥﴾}$$

5. But, what can make you really understand *al- Ḥuṭamah?*

By asking this question, Allaah is really telling us that *al-Ḥuṭamah* is too much for man's mind to understand. This creature of Allaah is beyond the imagination. It should be feared and avoided. There is nothing in this world which is like it. Even the atomic bomb which has the power to crush and destroy can not be compared to *al-Ḥuṭmah*. No man in his right mind who has understood what Allaah is saying here would want to meet *al-Ḥuṭamah*. This verse strikes fear in the hearts of the Believers and encourages them to do as much good as they can. Because, it is only true belief and good deeds which will protect man from *al-Ḥuṭamah*.

$$\text{نَارُ ٱللَّهِ ٱلْمُوقَدَةُ ﴿٦﴾}$$

6. It is the blazing fire of Allaah

Here, Allaah explains just exactly what *al-Ḥuṭamah* is. It is simply one of the names of the Hell-fire. The name helps us to understand some of the effects of the Fire. This is important because there is no way for us to understand the Hell-fire. It is a living creature created by Allaah. It breathes, sighs and speaks. Allaah describes the Hell fire in the Qur'aan as follows:

$$\text{إِذَآ أُلْقُوا۟ فِيهَا سَمِعُوا۟ لَهَا شَهِيقًا وَهِىَ تَفُورُ}$$

"When they are cast in, they will hear the drawing in of its breath as it blazes forth."

(Soorah al-Mulk (67):7)

-68-

$$\text{يَوْمَ نَقُولُ لِجَهَنَّمَ هَلِ ٱمْتَلَأْتِ وَتَقُولُ هَلْ مِن مَّزِيدٍ}$$

"One day we will ask Hell, 'Are you full?' It will answer, 'Is there more?' "

(Soorah Qaaf (50):30)

The flames of this world are nothing compared to *al-Ḥutamah*. They are chemical reactions which burn for a while then die out, but the Hell-fire is eternal. Its flames never die out and its heat is so great that it burns things right out of existence.

Allaah refers to it as "His fire" to let us know that it is a very special fire. All fires are Allaah's, because it is He who has created them, and it is He who has given them the power to burn. But, the Hell-fire is not of this world. It has been specially prepared as a punishment for the wicked in the next world.

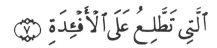

7. Which overcomes the hearts.

This Fire is so powerful that its burning flames reach into the human body and grab the heart in its fiery hands. A man's heart is the most private thing which he owns. It is where he keeps his secrets hidden from all of those around him. And all the decisions of his life take place there. Therefore, his heart is the home of his disbelief in Allaah. So the severe punishment which awaits those who slander Allaah will reach every inch of their bodies. Even their souls will be on fire. And there will be no break.

$$\text{إِنَّهَا عَلَيْهِم مُّؤْصَدَةٌ} \ \textcircled{8} \ \text{فِى عَمَدٍ مُّمَدَّدَةٍ} \ \textcircled{9}$$

8. Verily it will be closed tightly over them. 9. In columns stretching outward.

The Fire will be sealed shut on top of them and will take the form of tubes of flames. They will be trapped in the centers of these fiery columns and they will be neither dead nor alive. Allaah says of those in Hell:

$$فَإِنَّ لَهُۥ جَهَنَّمَ لَا يَمُوتُ فِيهَا وَلَا يَحۡيَىٰ$$

"For him is Hell in which he will neither die nor live"

(Soorah Taa Haa (20):74)

But they will continually feel death coming. Allaah says:

$$وَيَأۡتِيهِ ٱلۡمَوۡتُ مِن كُلِّ مَكَانٍ وَمَا هُوَ بِمَيِّتٍ$$

"And death will come to him from everywhere, yet he will not die..."

(Soorah Ibraaheem (14):17)

In this state between life and death they will remain forever. Such will be the end of all those who slander Allaah, His Prophets, His Books and the Believers.

Summary

Allaah has described the end of the slanderers in detail in order to scare those among them who might listen. And He also did it to remind the Believers that their enemies would not escape Allaah's punishment. This reminder would naturally encourage the Believers to make more sacrifices for Allaah's religion, al-Islaam. And it would also give them courage to be patient in the times of difficulty which they all must face.

QUESTIONS

The name *Humazah* means
    (a) Allaah's help or aid.
    (b) a greedy person who hoards wealth
    (c) a salamander.
    (d) one who tells lies about people.
    (e) the Hell-fire.

2. Explain the difference between slander and backbiting.

3. In order to show how strongly Islaam is opposed to backbiting
    (a) Allaah set the punishment of ninety lashes for anyone caught backbiting.
    (b) Allaah declared that backbiters will be destroyed by *al-Huṭamah*.
    (c) Allaah compared it in the Qur'aan to eating the flesh of one's dead brother.
    (d) The Qur'aan states that Allaah will not forgive those who backbite.
    (e) Islamic law has set the punishment of one hundred lashes for those who backbite women.

4. The most serious form of slander is
    (a) backbiting decent women.
    (b) to make fun of the believers.
    (c) to tell lies about the Prophet (ﷺ).
    (d) eating the flesh of one's dead brother.
    (e) to slander Allaah by claiming that He does not exist.

5. Verse. 2 **"Who gathered wealth and counted it."**
    (a) Why does the slanderer spend most of his time gathering wealth?
    (b) How does the slanderer look at his wealth and the poverty of others?
    (c) What is the real purpose of wealth?

6. Give an example of how the disbelievers of the past believed their wealth would make them immortal.

7. Al-Ḥuṭamah is

   (a) a beast from paradise which crushes the believers on the Day of Judgement.
   (b) one who slanders and backbites people.
   (c) one of the names of the Day of Judgement.
   (d) one of the names of the Hell-fire.
   (e) an uncle of the Prophet (ﷺ) who used to make fun of him.

8. Describe two qualities of the Hellfire which show that it is different from the fires of this world.

9. Verse 7. **"Which overcomes the hearts"**

This verse refers to:

   (a) disbelief which takes over the hearts of the disbelievers.
   (b) sorrow which overcomes disbelievers when they die.
   (c) happiness which fills the hearts of those going to paradise.
   (d) the Hellfire's destruction of the souls of those placed in it.
   (e) death coming to disbelievers in this life.

10. Explain three reasons why Allaah describes in detail the punishment of the slanderers.

8. USOOL AL-ḤADEETH

Ḥadeeth literally means a saying or conversation, but Islamically it represents the sayings and actions of the Prophet Muḥammad (ﷺ) related by his companions and collected in books by those scholars who came after them. The following is an example of what a *Ḥadeeth* looks like:

حَدَّثَنَا مُسَدَّدٌ قَالَ حَدَّثَنا يَحْيٰ عَنْ شُعْبَةَ عَنْ قَتَادَةَ عَنْ أَنَسٍ عَنِ النَّبِيِّ ﷺ قَالَ : «لاَ يُؤْمِنُ أَحَدُكُمْ حَتّى يُحِبَّ لأِخْيهِ مَايُحِبُّ لِنَفْسِهِ» رَوَاهُ الْبُخَارِيُّ .

Musaddad told us that Yaḥyaa informed him from Shuʻbah, from Qataadah, from Anas from the Prophet (ﷺ) that he said:

"None of you truly believes until he loves for his brother what he loves for himself."

Collected by al-Bukhaaree[1]

This means that the *Ḥadeeth* scholar Muḥammad ibn Ismaaʻeel al-Bukhaaree collected in his book of *Ḥadeeths* called *Saheeh al-Bukhaaree* the statement: *"None of you truly believes until he loves for his brother what he loves for himself."* which he heard from his *Ḥadeeth* teacher Musaddad, who heard it from his teacher Yaḥyaa, who was informed by his teacher Shuʻbah that he heard it from his teacher Qataadah, a student of the Prophet's (ﷺ) companion, who heard it quoted by the companions Anas ibn Maalik from the Prophet (ﷺ).

THE STRUCTURE OF ḤADEETH

A *Ḥadeeth* consists of two main parts: the *Sanad* (السند) and the *Matn* (المتن).

---

[1] *(Sahih Al-Bukhari* (Arabic-English), vol. 1, p. 19, no. 12). It is also collected by Muslim *(Sahih Muslim* (English Trans.), vol. 1, p. 31, no. 72).

The Sanad

The list of the narrators of the saying or action of the Prophet (ﷺ) is called the *Sanad*. For example, in the above *Hadeeth* the *Sanad* is: "Musaddad told us that Yahyaa informed him from Shu'bah from Qataadah from Anas from the Prophet (ﷺ) that he said:"

The Matn

The text of the *Hadeeth* or what the Prophet (ﷺ) actually said or did is called the *Matn*. For example, in the above *Hadeeth* the *Matn* is: "None of you truly believes until he loves for his brother what he loves for himself."

CLASSES OF HADEETH

Hadeeth are divided into two main categories: *Hadeeth Saheeh* and *Hadeeth Da'eef*.

The Hadeeth Saheeh

If all of the narrators in the *Sanad* fulfill the following three conditions, the *Hadeeth* is classified as an accurate saying or action of the Prophet (ﷺ) and named *Saheeh*. This means that we can be certain that the Prophet (ﷺ) actually said or did what was reported in the *Hadeeth*.

(1) The narrators must all be known to be truthful.

(2) They must all have had good memories, or have written down what they heard.[1]

(3) They must all have met each other.

Such a *Hadeeth* can be used to prove a point of Islamic Law which should be followed. The *Hadeeth* are the second most important

---

[1] Scholars later graded the memories of narrators into excellent and acceptable. If all had excellent memories the *Hadeeth* was rated *Saheeh*, and if some were acceptable it was rated *Hasan*. However, both categories are considered authentic.

source of Islamic Law and all true Muslims must follow them. Allaah in the Qur'aan said,

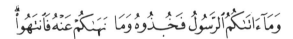

"Whatever the messenger gives you, you should accept and whatever he forbids you, you should reject."
(Soorah al-Ḥashr (59):7)

The only way that we can follow that command of God is to learn the *Ḥadeeth* of the Prophet (ﷺ) and put them into practice.

The *Ḥadeeth* mentioned at the beginning of the chapter is a *Ḥadeeth Saheeh* which teaches Muslims about Faith *(Eemaan)*. True belief in God will cause the believer to treat others well especially their brothers in faith. Human beings naturally want to be treated nicely, as such, good treatment is an important part of a comfortable and pleasant life. It develops love, trust, respect and many other good characteristics among people. In order to establish good human relations, Islaam encourages Muslims to treat others in the same good manner in which they would like to be treated by others.

Al-Bukhaaree collected from Muhammad ibn al-Muthannaa, from 'Abdul-Wahhaab, from Ayyoob from Abu Qilaabah, from Maalik that the Prophet (ﷺ) said, *"Pray as you have seen me praying."*[1] This *Ḥadeeth* fulfills the above-mentioned conditions and is therefore *Saheeh*. The point of Islamic law in it is that in formal prayer *(Salaah)* we must follow the method used by the Prophet (ﷺ). Muslims are not allowed to make up their own personal style of prayer, as it is not only disobedience to the Prophet (ﷺ) but it will also lead to confusion in the prayer lines. The correct description of the Prophet's (ﷺ) *Salaah* can be found in the books of *Ḥadeeth*. So we must read and find out how the Prophet (ﷺ) prayed in order to follow him properly.

---

[1] *Sahih Al-Bukhari* (Arabic-English), vol. 1, p. 345, no. 604

The Hadeeth Da'eef

If any of the narrators in the *Sanad* were known to have had any of the following faults, the *Hadeeth* is then classified as being inaccurate and referred to as *Da'eef*.

1. If any were known to have been liars.

2. If any were known to have had bad memories.

3. If any were known to have not met the one he was supposed to be narrating from.

The *Hadeeth Da'eef* is not a true saying or action of the Prophet (ﷺ) and cannot be used to prove any point of Islamic Law. Any law which is based on such a *Hadeeth* is considered incorrect. For example, *Hadeeth* scholars Abu Daawood and Ahmad collected a narration from Hafs ibn Ghayyaath who reported from 'Abdur-Rahmaan ibn Is-haaq from Ziyaad ibn Zayd from Abu Juhayfah that 'Alee ibn Abee Taalib was supposed to have said, "The *Sunnah* position of hands in *Salaah* is to place one hand on the other hand, below the navel." However, this *Hadeeth* is classified as *Da'eef* because 'Abdur-Rahmaan was a known liar. Therefore, it can not be used to support the practice of placing one's hands below the navel in *Salaah*. The correct practice is as *Taawoos* reported in another *Hadeeth* which is *Saheeh*. He said that Allaah's Messenger (ﷺ) used to put his right hand on his left hand and place them on his chest whenever he was in *Salaah*. This *Hadeeth* was also collected by Abu Daawood and Ahmad as well as Ibn Khuzaymah. Of course, the placing of one's hands below the navel or on the navel does not ruin one's *Salaah*.

Al-Hasan ibn 'Ateeyah reported from Abu 'Aatikah from Anas that the Prophet (ﷺ) said, "Seek knowledge even in China." This *Hadeeth* was collected by the *Hadeeth* scholars Ibn 'Adee and Abu

---

[1] *Sunan Abu Dawud* (English Trans.), vol. 1, p. 194, no. 756.

[2] *Sunan Abu Dawud* (English Trans.), vol. 1, p. 194, no. 757, and rated *Saheeh* by al-Albaanee in *Saheeh Sunan Abee Daawood*, vol. 1, p. 144, no. 687.

Nu'aym. Although it is a commonly quoted *Hadeeth* which is well known among Muslims, it is <u>not</u> accurate. Abu 'Aatikah was accused of falsifying *Hadeeths*, thus this narration is classified as *Da'eef*. In fact, *Hadeeth* scholars have put it in a special category of *Da'eef Hadeeths* called *Mawdoo'* (fabricated). Consequently it is incorrect to quote this statement as a *Hadeeth* of the Prophet (ﷺ), because many of his companions have quoted him as saying, *"Let whoever deliberately lies about me take his seat in the Hellfire."*[1]

The most famous books of *Hadeeths* are called "the Sound Six" *(as-Sihaah as-Sittah)*. They are Saheeh al-Bukhaaree, Saheeh Muslim, Sunan Abu Dawood, Sunan at-Tirmidhee, Sunan an-Nasaa'ee and Sunan Ibn Maajah. The oldest collection of *Hadeeths* to reach us is the *Muwatta'* of Maalik and the largest collection of *Hadeeths* is the *Musnad* of Ahmad. The most accurate collection of *Hadeeths* is that of al-Bukhaaree and the second most accurate is that of Muslim. That is, one may freely quote *Hadeeths* from both the Saheehs of al-Bukhaaree and Muslim as evidence, because they are very nearly all authentic. However, the other books of *Hadeeths* contain a number of inaccurate narrations which cannot be used as evidence. Therefore, only the *Hadeeths* which have been rated accurate by the scholars may be used from the other books. It should also be noted that most modern books only mention the last narrator before the Prophet (ﷺ) when quoting *Hadeeths* in order to save time and space.

---

[1] Narrated by 'Alee ibn Abee Taalib, Ibn 'Abbaas, Abu Sa'eed al-Khudree, 'Abdullaah ibn 'Amr, Abu Hurayrah, Ibn Mas'ood, al-Mugheerah ibn Shu'bah and az-Zubayr, and collected by al-Bukhaaree and Muslim as well as most other collectors of *Hadeeths*.

QUESTIONS

1. *Hadeeth* may be defined as
   (a) the sayings and actions of God narrated by the Prophet (ﷺ) and written down in books by the **companions**.
   (b) the sayings of the Prophet (ﷺ) which he wrote down for his companions.
   (c) the actions of the Prophet's (ﷺ) companions written down in books by scholars who came after them.
   (d) the sayings and actions of the Prophet (ﷺ) narrated by his companions and collected in books by later scholars.
   (e) the sayings and actions of the Prophet (ﷺ) collected in books by his companions and narrated by later scholars who came after them.

2. The *Sanad* of the *Hadeeth* is
   (a) the chain of companions who observed the Prophet's (ﷺ) saying or action.
   (b) the list of sayings of the Prophet (ﷺ) narrated by the *Matn*.
   (c) a group of narrators who witnessed the Prophet's (ﷺ) sayings or actions.
   (d) the chain of narrators of the saying or action of the Prophet (ﷺ)
   (e) the list of sayings or actions of the companions of the Prophet (ﷺ)

3. (a) What are three (3) differences between a *Hadeeth Saheeh* and a *Hadeeth Da'eef?*

   (b) How can these two types of *Hadeeths* be used in Islamic law?

   (c) Explain why the correct position for placing the hands in *Salaah* is on the chest and not below the navel.

4. The two most accurate books of *Hadeeth* are those of
   (a) Al-Bukhaaree and at-Tirmidhee.
   (b) Muslim and Ibn Maajah.
   (c) Abu Daawood and an-Nasaa'ee.

(d) Muslim and al-Bukhaaree.

(e) Al-Bukhaaree and an-Nasaa'ee.

5. (a) Which is the oldest book of *Hadeeths* to reach us.?

(b) What are "the Sound Six"?

(c) Which *Hadeeth* book contains the largest number of *Hadeeths?*

6. .*Hadeeths* may be freely quoted as evidence from the *Sunans* and other books of *Hadeeth*

(a) because nearly all of *Hadeeths* in them are authentic.

(b) only if they are rated accurate by the scholars of *Hadeeth*.

(c) because all *Hadeeths* are from the Prophet (ﷺ) and Allaah said we must do whatever he tells us.

(d) if they are reported by Anas ibn Maalik.

(e) only if they are classified *Da'eef* by the *Hadeeth* scholars.

7. The *Hadeeth* "Seek knowledge even in China" is

(a) a *Saheeh Hadeeth*.

(b) found in *Sunan Abu Daawood*.

(c) not authentic.

(d) proof that seeking knowledge is compulsory.

(e) reported by al-Bukhaaree and Muslim.

9. ḤADEETH ONE: GOOD CHARACTER

عَنِ النَّوَّاسِ بْنِ سَمْعَانَ عَنِ النَّبِيِّ ﷺ قَالَ: «الَبِرُّ حُسْنُ الْخُلُقِ وَالإِثْمُ
مَاحَاكَ فِي نَفْسِكَ وَكَرِهْتَ أَن يَطَّلِعَ عَلَيْهِ النَّاسُ» رَوَاهُ مُسْلِمٌ

An-Nawwaas ibn Sam'aan reported that the Prophet (ﷺ) said: "Righteousness is good character and sin is whatever bothers you and you do not want people to know about."

Collected by Muslim[1]

The Narrator

An-Nawwaas ibn Sam'aan was a famous *Ṣaḥaabee* (companion of the Prophet (ﷺ) from the tribe of Kallaab who settled in Syria after the death of the Prophet (ﷺ).

The Collector

Muslim's full name was Muslim ibn al-Ḥajjaaj Al-Qushayree. He was born in 817 C.E. in the city of Nishapur which is in the north eastern part of Iran near the city of Meshed. Muslim began the study of *Ḥadeeth* at the age of 15 and travelled to Iraq, Ḥijaaz, (western coast of Arabia), Syria and Egypt in order to study under great scholars of *Ḥadeeth* like al-Bukhaaree, Aḥmad ibn Ḥambal, 'Abd ibn Ḥumayd and Ibn Abee Shaybah. He later had many students who went on to become great scholars after his death. Among the most famous of his students were at-Tirmidhee and Ibn Abee Ḥaatim.

Muslim compiled a *Ḥadeeth* book containing 9,200 *Ḥadeeths* which he called *al-Musnad as-Ṣaheeh*, but which later became known as *Ṣaheeh Muslim*. *Ṣaheeh Muslim* is considered by most Muslim scholars to be

---

[1] *Sahih Muslim* (English Trans.), vol. 4, p. 1358-9, no. 6196.

the most accurate book of *Hadeeth* after that of al-Bukhaaree. It has been translated into English by Abdul Hamid Siddiqui and was published in four volumes in Pakistan in the year 1976. Imaam Muslim died in the city of his birth in the year 875 C.E. at the early age of 58, but left to all the generations of Muslims who came after him a great contribution to Islaam.

GENERAL MEANING

This *Hadeeth* of the Prophet (ﷺ) teaches us that good character (i.e. kindness, politeness, truthfulness, etc.) is the most important part of what Islaam calls "Righteousness". This means that it is not possible for someone to be considered truly righteous and be of bad character. People often think of being righteous as simply doing religious deeds like *Salaah* and *Zakaah*. But, these religious acts are meant to build good character. Allaah says:

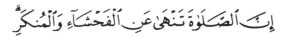

"Surely *Salaah* prevents evil speech and evil deeds"
(Soorah al-'Ankaboot (29):45)

The Prophet (ﷺ) himself said: *"Surely, I was only sent to complete the most noble character traits."*[1] And Allaah said in the Qur'aan,

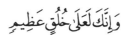

"Surely you (Muhammad) have great character"
(Soorah al-Qalam (68):4)

And when the Prophet's wife 'Aa'eshah was asked about the Prophet's (ﷺ) character, she replied, *"His (ﷺ) character was that of the*

---

[1] Narrated by Abu Hurayrah and collected by al-Bukhaaree in al-Adab al-Mufrad, al-Haakim and al-Bayhaqee in *Shu'ab al-Eemaan*. Authenticated by al-Albaanee in *Saheeh al-Jaami' as-Sagheer*, vol. 1, p. 464, no. 2349.

Qur'aan."[1] That is, his manners were according to Allaah's instructions in the Qur'aan. Consequently, if we wish to develop good character, we should follow closely the Qur'aan and the teachings of the Prophet (ﷺ). Allaah also said in the Qur'aan

$$لَّقَدْ كَانَ لَكُمْ فِى رَسُولِ ٱللَّهِ أُسْوَةٌ حَسَنَةٌ$$

"Indeed you have in the Messenger of Allaah a beautiful example (of conduct)…"

(Soorah al-Ahzaab (33):21)

So we cannot separate Islaam from good manners. Islaam teaches man how to lead a righteous life by pointing out the proper way to live. Any Muslim who displays bad manners such as swearing or lying is either a hypocrite pretending to be a Muslim or a really very weak Muslim.

Islaam teaches great respect for parents and elders as a very important part of good character. Allaah said,

$$وَقَضَىٰ رَبُّكَ أَلَّا تَعْبُدُوٓا۟ إِلَّآ إِيَّاهُ وَبِٱلْوَٰلِدَيْنِ إِحْسَٰنًا ۚ إِمَّا يَبْلُغَنَّ عِندَكَ ٱلْكِبَرَ أَحَدُ$$

$$هُمَآ أَوْ كِلَاهُمَا فَلَا تَقُل لَّهُمَآ أُفٍّ وَلَا تَنْهَرْهُمَا وَقُل لَّهُمَا قَوْلًا كَرِيمًا$$

"Your Lord has ordered that you only worship Him and that you be kind to (your) parents. Whether one or both of them reach old age with you, do not say any harsh word to them nor push them away. Speak to them in kind terms."

(Soorah al-Israa' (7):23)

The Prophet (ﷺ) also said, *"Whoever is not kind to our young ones*

---

[1] Collected by Muslim *(Sahih Muslim* (English Trans.), vol. 1, pp. 358-360, no. 1623), Abu Daawood, *(Sunan Abu Dawud* (English Trans.), vol. 1, pp. 351-2, no. 1337) and Ahmad. Authenticated by al-Albaanee in *Saheeh Sunan Abee Daawood* vol. 1, pp. 249-250, no. 1193.

and respectful to our elders is not of us."[1] So, one can not be a truly good Muslim unless he treats his parents and elders properly by obeying them and speaking to them nicely.

The *Hadeeth* also teaches that we have been given a means of judging good and bad which is inside ourselves. Allaah has made it a part of our nature. Allaah said,

فَأَلْهَمَهَا فُجُورَهَا وَتَقْوَىٰهَا

"He inspired it (the soul) to know its sin and its piety"

(Soorah ash-Shams (91):8)

If something pleases us and we have no doubts about it in our hearts, we can consider it to be good. That is, as long as it does not go against any of the laws of Islaam. But, if something creates doubts in our hearts and we would not like others to know that we were even thinking about it, we should avoid it and know that it is bad. On one occasion a man came to the Prophet (ﷺ) to ask him about righteousness and he told him, *"Ask your heart."*[2] The Prophet (ﷺ) is telling us that if we listen to our hearts we will all be guided to the truth. It could therefore be said that the main message of this *Hadeeth* is that righteousness is a characteristic which all true Muslims should have. And, everyone has the ability to be righteous if only they would be honest with themselves.

Lessons

1. We should try to develop good character.

2. Good character is among the greatest forms of righteousness.

3. We should avoid doubtful things.

4. We should also listen to our hearts.

---

[1] Narrated by Anas and collected by at-Tirmidhee, and rated *Saheeh* by al-Albaanee in *Saheeh al-Jaami' as-Sagheer*, vol. 1, p. 958, no. 958, no. 5445.

[2] Narrated by Waabisah and collected by Ahmad and ad-Daarimee, and rated authentic *(Hasan)* by al-Albaanee in *Mishkaah al-Masaabeeh*, vol. 2, p. 845, no. 2774.

QUESTIONS

1. Mention four points about the collector of this *Ḥadeeth*.

2. The Prophet's (ﷺ) statement *"Righteousness is good charac-*
   ter" means that
   (a) one can not be righteous without doing some bad deeds.
   (b) good character is not an important part of righteousness.
   (c) one must have good character to be truly righteous.
   (d) bad character is a sign of righteousness.
   (e) nothing is righteous except good character.

3. Briefly mention why good manners can not be separated from
   Islaam.

4. Explain what the Prophet (ﷺ) said about treating those who are
   younger than us and those older.

5. Why should younger people greet older people first and not the
   other way around?

6. We are able to judge between right and wrong
   (a) if we follow our conscience and avoid doubtful acts.
   (b) by following our desires and doing whatever we want to do.
   (c) if we do only the things we enjoy doing.
   (d) by choosing to do only the things in which we have doubt.
   (e) if we always listen to the advice of our friends.

7. This *Ḥadeeth* encourages us to
   (a) develop doubts about our friends and family.
   (b) avoid people who are too righteous.
   (c) make excuses for our bad character.
   (d) develop good character.
   (e) treat only those people whom we like nicely.

10. HADEETH TWO: SUSPICION

عَنْ أَبِى هُرَيْرَةَ أَنَّ رَسُوْلَ الله ﷺ قَالَ : «إِيَّاكُمْ وَالظَّنَّ فَإِنَّ الظَّنَّ أَكْذَبُ الْحَدِيْثِ» رَوَاهُ الْبُخَارِىُّ و مُسْلِمُ

Abu Hurayrah reported that Allaah's Messenger said; "Beware of suspicion, for verily suspicion is the most misleading form of conversation."

Collected by both al-Bukhaaree and Muslim[1]

Narrator

Abu Hurayrah's real name was 'Abdur-Rahmaan ibn Sakhr. He was born in Yemen, but travelled to Madeenah to accept Islaam from the Prophet (ﷺ) himself. The Prophet (ﷺ) later nicknamed him Abu Hurayrah because he often used to carry a little kitten in his arms. *Hirrah* means cat and *Hurayrah* means a kitten while Abu means "father of" or "owner of". Thus, Abu Hurayrah literally means owner of the kitten.

Abu Hurayrah narrated 1,236 *Hadeeths* from the Prophet (ﷺ) which was more than any other companion of the Prophet (ﷺ). He died in Madeenah and was buried there in the year 59 A.H./679 C.E. at the age of 78.

Collector

Al-Bukhaaree's full name at the time of his birth in 810 C.E. was Muhammad ibn Ismaa'eel. He was called al-Bukhaaree because he was born in in the city of Bukhaaraa which is now in the south eastern

---

[1] *Sahih Muslim* (English Trans.), vol. 4, p. 1361, no. 6214, *Sahih Al-Bukhari* (Arabic-English), vol. 8, p. 58, no. 90 and *(Sunan Abu Dawud* (English Trans.), vol. 3, p. 1370, no. 4899.

Russian state of Uzbekistan. Imaam Bukhaaree began his study of *Hadeeth* from the early age of 10. His father, Ismaa'eel was himself a scholar of *Hadeeth*, who had studied the subject under some very famous scholars such as Maalik ibn Anas and Hammaad ibn Zayd. Al-Bukhaaree travelled all over the Muslim world collecting *Hadeeths* and composed his famous collection of *Hadeeths* which he called *Al-Jaami' al-Musnad as-Saheeh*, but which later became known as *Saheeh al-Bukhaaree*. *Saheeh al-Bukhaaree* contained 2,602 *Hadeeths* which he chose from the many thousands that he had memorized. He died in Samarkand, the present day capital of Uzbekistan, in the year 870 C.E. at the age of 60. *Saheeh al-Bukhaaree* is considered by Muslim scholars to be the most authentic book in Islaam after Qur'aan. *Saheeh al-Bukhaaree* has been translated into English by Muhammad Muhsin Khan. It was published in 1976 by the Islamic University of Madeenah.

Imaam Muslim's biography can be found in *Hadeeth* No. 1.

GENERAL MEANING

In the Qur'aan Allaah has set down for Muslims general guidelines concerning suspicion. He stated:

$$ اجْتَنِبُوا كَثِيرًا مِنَ الظَّنِّ إِنَّ بَعْضَ الظَّنِّ إِثْمٌ $$

"Avoid a lot of suspicion, for verily some suspicion is sin."

(Soorah al-Hujuraat (49):12).

Suspicion based on evidence is natural and allowable. For example, if something was missing from someone's school bag and one student was known to have been alone in the classroom, he would naturally be a suspect. But one must avoid excesses in suspicion. A true Muslim is not overly suspicious. He does not judge all those around him guilty until proven innocent. Such excesses always lead to corruption. Often a person who is overly suspicious will openly express his opinion about others by accusing them with little or no evidence. And by doing that he falls into the grave sin of slander.

The Prophet (ﷺ) in this *Hadeeth* confirmed Allaah's warning to avoid a lot of suspicion by telling us to be very careful when dealing with suspicion whether in large or small quantities. He then went on to explain why extreme caution must be taken. When suspicion is spoken about, it becomes the most deceptive form of conversation. It often fools both the one expressing it, as well as the one who hears it, because it often carries with it the possibility of being true. The one who raises the suspicion does not feel that he is lying because he is only expressing a thought. The one who hears it then develops suspicion. He, in turn, passes the suspicion on to others and others to others. And, that is how rumours are born and spread.

As long as a suspicion remains a thought, its owner is not held to account for it. The Prophet (ﷺ) said in another *Hadeeth* that *"Allaah overlooks the bad thoughts of the Muslim nation as long as they do not speak about it or act on it."*[1] Therefore, a suspicious person is held to account for his suspicion only when suspicion leaves the world of thought and becomes an action, whether spoken or done.

Islaam despises suspicion from another point of view also. Slander, backbiting and gossip can only take root and grow if suspicion is present. That is, if you are suspicious of someone and you hear a bad story about him, you would be more likely to believe it than if you were not suspicious. Therefore, because suspicion is often the breeding ground for other negative qualities, Islaam opposes it even in the realm of thought by encouraging us to avoid a lot of it.

In order to help prevent suspicion from developing, the Prophet (ﷺ) said, *"When there are three persons, two should not converse secretly between themselves to the exclusion of the third one."*[2] The person who is excluded will probably be suspicious that the other two are talking about him. This type of suspicion is slightly different than the

---

[1] Collected by Muslim *(Sahih Muslim* (English Trans.), vol. 1, p. 74, no. 230).

[2] Reported by Ibn 'Umar and collected by al-Bukhaaree, Muslim *(Sahih Muslim* (English Trans.), vol. 3, p. 1191, no. 5419) and Abu Daawood *(Sunan Abu Dawud* (English Trans.), vol. 3, p. 1354, no. 4834).

other, but they both involve bad thoughts about people, which is not good.

The *Hadeeth* of the chapter is only the beginning of a longer *Hadeeth*. The Prophet (ﷺ) went on to say, *"And do not be inquisitive about one another, nor spy on each other. And do not feel envy, dislike, hatred or hostility towards each other. Instead, be brothers and servants of Allaah together."* This remaining part of the Prophet's (ﷺ) statement describes many of the bad effects of suspicion on the Islamic brotherhood. So the Prophet (ﷺ) ended by calling us to the brotherhood of faith about which Allaah said,

$$\text{إِنَّمَا ٱلْمُؤْمِنُونَ إِخْوَةٌ فَأَصْلِحُوا بَيْنَ أَخَوَيْكُمْ}$$

"Certainly the believers are one brotherhood so make peace between your two (disagreeing) brothers."
(Soorah al-Ḥujuraat (49):10)

The greatest danger of suspicion is that it leads to the break-up of friendships and communities. Trust is destroyed by suspicion. And without trust there can be no friendships or community. Thus, Islaam stands opposed to suspicion by encouraging trust among Muslims. We should always think the best of others until they prove themselves otherwise. In that way, simple misunderstandings will not become the basis for hate and anger and the break-up of relationships.

Lessons

1. Suspicion must be avoided as much as possible.

2. Suspicion is the basis of rumours, slander and gossip which are all forbidden in Islaam.

3. Islaam is concerned with protecting the Muslim Community from habits which may break it up.

4. The quality which the Prophet (ﷺ) wanted us to develop in this *Hadeeth* is that of trust.

QUESTIONS

1. (a) What was al-Bukhaaree's full name?
   (b) Explain why he was called al-Bukhaaree.
   (c) What was he famous for?

2. What did Allaah say in the Qur'aan about suspicion?

3. Suspicion is natural and allowable
   (a) if it is based on evidence.
   (b) when you do not like someone.
   (c) if someone comes from another country.
   (d) when someone tells you something about someone else.
   (e) if you have lost something valuable.

4. One is held to account for suspicion
   (a) when it first enters our mind.
   (b) if it stays in our mind,
   (c) if we talk about it or act on it.
   (d) when it is not based on evidence.
   (e) if we hear it from others.

5. The Prophet (ﷺ) referred to suspicion as being the most misleading type of conversation because
   (a) all suspicions are lies.
   (b) suspicion leads to disbelief in God.
   (c) those who are suspicious of others will tell lies about them.
   (d) it tends to make both the one who expresses it as well as the
       one who hears it believe that it is the truth.
   (e) all suspicion is caused by Satan's whispering in man's ear.

6. Discuss the relationship between suspicion and rumours.

7. The greatest danger of suspicion is that it
   (a) leads to disbelief in God and evil deeds.
   (b) can cause a suspicious individual to think the best of others.
   (c) can not be controlled by most people.
   (d) often leads to the break-up of relationships and communities.

(e) never produces anything good.

8. Mention three ways by which Islaam overcomes this danger of suspicion.

11. HADEETH THREE: JEALOUSY

عَنْ أَبِى هُرَيْرَةَ أَنَّ النَّبِيَّ ﷺ قَالَ : «إِيَّاكُمْ وَالْحَسَدَ فَإِنَّ الْحَسَدَ يَأْكُلُ الْحَسَنَاتِ كَمَا تَأْكُلُ النَّارُ الْحَطَبَ» رَوَاهُ أَبُو دَاوُدَ

Abu Hurayrah reported that Allaah's messenger said, "Beware of jealousy for verily it destroys good deeds the way fire destroys wood."

Collected by Abu Daawood[1]

Narrator

Abu Hurayrah's biography can be found in *Hadeeth* Number 2.

Collector

Abu Daawood's full name was Sulaymaan ibn al-Ash'ath as-Sijis-taanee and he was born in the year 202 A.H./818 C.E. studied *Hadeeth* under Imaam Ahmad along with al-Bukhaaree and taught many of the later scholars of *Hadeeth*, like at-Tirmidhee and an-Nasaa'ee.

Abu Daawood selected 4,800 *Hadeeths* from over 500,000 which he had gathered and organized them in a book which he named *Sunan* [plural of *Sunnah* which means a practise of the Prophet (ﷺ)]. Abu Daawood taught his *Sunan* in Baghdaad and other major centers of Islaam of that time. He died in Basrah in the year 275 A.H./889 C.E.

The *Sunan* of Abu Daawood was translated into English by Ahmed Hasan in 1979. However, it was first published in three volumes by Sh. Muhammad Ashraf Publishers in 1984 in Pakistan.

GENERAL MEANING

Jealousy and envy are among the most destructive emotions or feel-

---

[1] *Sunan Abu Dawud* (English Trans.), vol. 3, p. 1366, no. 4855.

ings which a man may have. They lead him in his times of weakness to take the property of others unjustly or to refuse to help others when they are in need of help. It causes him to wish evil on others and to be happy when misfortune befalls them. Jealousy may also drive him to go beyond his means and squander his wealth in order to live like the wealthy. Jealousy also involves *Kufr*, (disbelief in Allaah) to a certain degree, because it causes the jealous individual to feel that Allaah has not been fair with him. He feels he deserves more than what Allaah has given him and forgets all the mercies Allaah has given him, without him even deserving them.

Allaah has deliberately given some people more wealth, intelligence, beauty, strength, children, etc., than others,

وَٱللَّهُ فَضَّلَ بَعْضَكُمْ عَلَىٰ بَعْضٍ فِى ٱلرِّزْقِ

"Allaah has favored some of you over others with sustenance."

(Soorah an-Nahl (16):71)

But He has forbidden us from desiring what others have,

وَلَا تَتَمَنَّوْاْ مَا فَضَّلَ ٱللَّهُ بِهِ بَعْضَكُمْ عَلَىٰ بَعْضٍ

"Do not wish for what we have favored some of you over others."

(Soorah an-Nisaa' (4):32)

Because these favors of Allaah are tests of faith. The more favors, the more tests. The material things of this life do not make one superior to another in Allaah's judgement. True superiority lies in faith in God. Allaah said,

إِنَّ أَكْرَمَكُمْ عِندَ ٱللَّهِ أَتْقَىٰكُمْ

"Surely the most noble of you to Allaah is the most God-fearing."

(Soorah al-Hujuraat (49):13)

In order to discourage envy the Prophet (ﷺ) said, *"Do not look to those above you. Look to those below you, as it will more likely remind you of Allaah's favors bestowed on you."*[1] This is in relation to the material things of this life as the Prophet (ﷺ) on another occasion said, *"If one of you looks at someone more wealthy and better built than him, he should also look at someone of a lower standard than himself."*[2] However, in spiritual matters we should look at those superior to us as it will encourage us to become more righteous. This is why the Prophet (ﷺ) said, *"Envy is only allowed in two cases: In the case of a man whom Allaah has given the Qur'aan and who recites it throughout the night and day; and a man on whom Allaah has bestowed wealth who gives it away throughout the night and day."*[3] In yet another narration of the same *Hadeeth* the Prophet (ﷺ) explained what may be said: *"I wish I were given what he was given and did with it what he did."*[4] So the jealousy is not merely in the gift but it also has to be in the correct use.

The Prophet (ﷺ) warned us to avoid envy as much as possible by comparing it to fire burning up wood completely, because envy and jealousy totally destroy whatever few good deeds we have done. In fact envy and jealousy are so dangerous that Allaah revealed a chapter of the Qur'aan to be recited as protection from those who envy us. In Soorah al-Falaq (113), Allaah said,

$$\text{وَمِن شَرِّ حَاسِدٍ إِذَا حَسَدَ} \qquad \text{قُلْ أَعُوذُ بِرَبِّ ٱلْفَلَقِ}$$

"Say: I seek refuge in the Lord of the dawn...from the evil of the envious when he envies."

---

[1] Reported by Abu Hurayrah and collected by al-Bukhaaree and Muslim *(Sahih Muslim* (English Trans.), vol. 4, p. 1530, no. 7070).

[2] *Sahih Muslim* (English Trans.), vol. 4, p. 1530, no. 7068.

[3] Reported by Ibn 'Umar and collected by al-Bukhaaree and Muslim.

[4] Reported by Abu Hurayrah and collected by al-Bukhaaree.

However, the main message of this *Hadeeth* is that believing Muslims should be content with what Allaah has destined for them. The Prophet (ﷺ) taught acceptance of fate as the sixth pillar of *Eemaan* (faith). This does not mean that the believer does not try to improve his situation. He or she should do their best in whatever circumstance they may be in. But, having done that, the believer should accept whatever Allaah destines for him.

Lessons

1. Islaam is concerned about removing negative emotions from people in order to bring about harmony and peace in society.

2. Jealousy is despised in Islaam, and Muslims should avoid it as much as possible.

3. Bad deeds destroy good deeds so it's not enough to do some good and think that we will automatically enter paradise because we are Muslim.

QUESTIONS

1. Mention four points about Abu Daawood.

2. The Prophet (ﷺ) warned us away from jealousy
   (a) to encourage us to work hard to get what others have.
   (b) because it makes us look down on others.
   (c) because it can cause people in times of weakness to commit sins.
   (d) to discourage us from trying to be the best.
   (e) to make us proud of what we have.

3. Give three examples of how jealousy could lead to sin.

4. Jealousy can become *Kufr*
   (a) if it makes you hate people.
   (b) if you feel that Allaah has been unfair to you.
   (c) when a person steals because of it.
   (d) because believers do not get jealous.
   (e) if one is happy when misfortune strikes others.

5. (a) When should we look to those above us and when should we not?
   (b) On what two occasions is jealousy allowed.

6. The Prophet (ﷺ) compared fire burning wood to jealousy
   (a) because the jealous person usually feels as if he is burning up.
   (b) to demonstrate how completely jealousy destroys good deeds.
   (c) because jealousy is such a major sin that it will cause those who experience it to go to the Hell-fire.
   (d) in order that Muslims would avoid the burning of wood due to jealousy.
   (e) to show how black the heart of a jealous person becomes.

7. What is the good characteristic that the Prophet (ﷺ) is encouraging us to develop in this *Hadeeth?*

12. HADEETH FOUR: PERMISSION

عَنْ كَلَدَةَ بْنِ حَنْبَلَ أَنَّ صَفْوَانَ بْنَ أُمَيَّةَ بَعَثَهُ بِلَبَنٍ وَلِبَأٍ وَ ضَغَابِيسَ إلَى النَّبِيِّ ﷺ وَالنَّبِيُّ ﷺ بِأَعْلَى الْوَادِي قَالَ : فَدَخَلْتُ عَلَيْهِ وَلَمْ أَسْتَأْذِنْ وَلَمْ أُسَلِّمْ فَقَالَ النَّبِيُّ ﷺ : «اِرْجِعْ فَقُلْ : اَلسَّلَامُ عَلَيْكُمْ أَأَدْخُلْ؟» رَوَاهُ التِّرْمِذِيُّ وَ أَبُودَاوُد

Kaladah ibn Hanbal reported that Safwaan ibn Umayyah sent him to the Prophet (ﷺ) with some milk and cucumbers when the Prophet (ﷺ) was staying in the upper part of the (Makkan) valley. He said, " I entered (his house) without seeking permission or giving *Salaams*, so the Prophet (ﷺ) said to me, 'Go back out and say: *as-Salaam 'alaykum*, may I enter?' "

Collected by Abu Daawood[1] and at-Tirmidhee

Narrator

Kaladah was from the tribe of Aslam and he accepted Islaam after the conquest of Makkah and the battle of Hunayn. He was a *Sahaabee* and among those who taught the *Sunnah* to new converts after the Prophet's (ﷺ) death.

Collector

Abu Daawood's biography can be found in *Hadeeth* number 3.

At-Tirmidhee's full name was Muhammed ibn 'Eesaa ibn Saurah and he was born in Tirmidh which is now a town called Termez in the south of the Russian province called Uzbekistan very near the northern border of Afghanistan. He studied *Hadeeth* under Imaam al-Bukhaaree and Abu Daawood as well as their teachers.

---

[1] *Sunan Abu Dawud* (English Trans.), vol. 1, p. 1429, no. 5157. Rated *Saheeh* by al-Albaanee in *Saheeh Sunan Abee Daawood*, vol. 3, p. 972, no. 4311.

At-Tirmidhee composed a book of *Hadeeth* containing about 4,000 narrations which he named *al-Jaami'*, but which later became known as *Sunan at-Tirmidhee*. He also contributed greatly to the science of *Hadeeth* analysis and composed a book on it called *al-'Elal* after he had become blind. Muhammad ibn 'Eesaa died in Tirmidh in the year 267 A.H./881 C.E.

GENERAL MEANING

This story occurred when Kaladah's maternal brother, Safwaan ibn Umayyah sent him to the Prophet (ﷺ) with some milk and vegetables. Since Kaladah was new to Islaam and therefore needed guidance, the Prophet (ﷺ) instructed him on the proper manners for visiting.

The general method for visiting was already outlined in the Qur'aan. Allaah said,

$$ يَٰٓأَيُّهَاٱلَّذِينَ ءَامَنُوا۟ لَاتَدۡخُلُوا۟ بُيُوتًا غَيۡرَ بُيُوتِكُمۡ حَتَّىٰ تَسۡتَأۡنِسُوا۟ وَتُسَلِّمُوا۟ عَلَىٰٓ أَهۡلِهَاۚ $$

"O believers, do not enter houses other than your own until you have asked permission and given *Salaams* to those in them..."

(Soorah an-Noor (24):27)

This *Hadeeth* is an example of the Prophet (ﷺ) putting this Qur'anic verse into practice.

The reason why the giving of *Salaams* is necessary is to avoid surprising the host in a state of dress or undress in which he would not like to be seen. It is also to avoid catching the females of the house off-guard if any are present.

In order to prevent accidentally looking inside someone's home when the door is opened the Prophet (ﷺ) gave further advice on the way to stand. Huzayl said *"A man came to the Prophet's (ﷺ) door, stood facing it and asked permission to enter. The Prophet (ﷺ) said to him, " (Stand) away from it! (Stand) to this side or that. For surely seeking permission is to prevent the unlawful look."*[1] A young child may open the door before the household is prepared or the father may do so without checking the situation of his family properly. To avoid such accidents we are advised not to face the doorway directly when awaiting permission to enter, especially if the door is open. The Prophet (ﷺ) also sternly warned those who may have the urge to peep. Abu Hurayrah reported that Allaah's Messenger (ﷺ) said, *"Whoever peeps into a person's house without their permission and his eye is knocked out, has lost his eye without any claim to compensation."*[2] On one occasion a man peeped at the Prophet (ﷺ) while he was in his house and the Prophet (ﷺ) threw an arrowhead at him so he backed away.[3]

The Prophet (ﷺ) also disliked that a visitor not properly identify himself when asked. Jaabir went to the Prophet (ﷺ) to ask about his father's debt. He said, *"I knocked on the door. When he asked, 'Who is there?' I replied, 'It is I'. He repeated, 'I, I?' as if he disliked it."*[4]

In another *Hadeeth* reported by Abu Sa'eed al-Khudree the Prophet (ﷺ) described exactly how many times the *Salaams* and request for entry should be given. He reported that the Prophet (ﷺ) said,

---

[1] Collected by Abu Daawood *(Sunan Abu Dawud* (English Trans.), vol. 3, p. 1428, no. 5155) and rated *Saheeh* by al-Albaanee in *Saheeh Sunan Abee Daawood*, vol. 3, p. 972, no. 4310.)

[2] Collected by Abu Daawood *(Sunan Abu Dawud* (English Trans.), vol. 3, p. 1428, no. 5153). Rated *Saheeh* in *Saheeh Sunan Abee Daawood*, vol. 3, p. 972, no. 4309.

[3] Related by Anas and collected by at-Tirmidhee and rated *Saheeh* in *Saheeh Sunan at-Tirmidhee*, vol. 2, p. 348, no. 2178.

[4] Collected by Abu Daawood *(Sunan Abu Dawud* (English Trans.), vol. 3, p. 1431, no. 5168) and rated *Saheeh* in *Saheeh Sunan Abee Daawood*, vol. 3, p. 974, no. 3419.

"When anyone of you seeks permission (to enter) three times and he is not granted permission, he should return."[1]

Allaah has given further instructions for privacy within the household. He said,

بَيَٰٓأَيُّهَا ٱلَّذِينَ ءَامَنُوا۟ لِيَسْتَـٔذِنكُمُ ٱلَّذِينَ مَلَكَتْ أَيْمَـٰنُكُمْ وَٱلَّذِينَ لَمْ يَبْلُغُوا۟ ٱلْحُلُمَ مِنكُمْ ثَلَـٰثَ مَرَّٰتٍ مِّن قَبْلِ صَلَوٰةِ ٱلْفَجْرِ وَحِينَ تَضَعُونَ ثِيَابَكُم مِّنَ ٱلظَّهِيرَةِ وَمِنۢ بَعْدِ صَلَوٰةِ ٱلْعِشَآءِ ثَلَـٰثُ عَوْرَٰتٍ لَّكُمْ لَيْسَ عَلَيْكُمْ وَلَا عَلَيْهِمْ جُنَاحٌۢ بَعْدَهُنَّ طَوَّٰفُونَ عَلَيْكُم بَعْضُكُمْ عَلَىٰ بَعْضٍ

"Oh you who believe! let those whom your right hands possess, and your (children) who have not reached puberty ask permission (before) they come in your presence on three occasions: before the morning prayer (Ṣalaatul-Fajr), when you remove your clothes from the midday heat, and after the late-night prayer (Ṣalaatul-'Ishaa). These are your three times of undress. Outside of these times it is not wrong for you or for them to move about."

(Soorah an-Noor (24):58)

Thus, even among members of the same household, permission has to be sought at times when people are usually in a state of undress.

This *Ḥadeeth* of this chapter shows the great care which Islaam has given to even the simplest of matters in order that there be guidance and a system of conduct for all occasions in life. If no instruction were left in this area, a visitor may easily offend his host by catching him or his family in a state of undress or by finding his place in a mess. He may also continue to ring the door bell for a long period of time, thereby making a nuisance of himself.

---

[1] Collected by Muslim *(Sahih Muslim* (English Trans.), vol. 3, p. 1175-6, no. 5354) and Abu Daawood *(Sunan Abu Dawud* (English Trans.), vol. 3, p. 429-430, no. 5161).

Lessons

1. Muslims are obliged to give *Salaams* and seek permission before entering other people's houses.

2. New people in Islaam should be instructed in the areas in which they are ignorant.

3. The system of Islaam covers all the areas of life and protects people from accidentally offending each other.

Questions

1. (a) Mention at-Tirmidhee's actual name and explain where the name at-Tirmidhee came from.

   (b) Who were his two main teachers?

   (c) What is *al-'Elal?*

2. Why did Kaladah enter the Prophet's (ﷺ) house without giving *Salaams?*
   (a) Because he was in a hurry.
   (b) In order to see what was going on inside without the Prophet (ﷺ) knowing.
   (c) Because he had already knocked on the door.
   (d) Kaladah was new to Islaam and did not know it was necessary.
   (e) Because he knew there were no women in the house.

3. The Prophet sent him back outside
   (a) in order to punish him for entering without permission.
   (b) to teach him the proper way of leaving someone's house.
   (c) because he was angry with him.
   (d) so that he could go back to his brother, Ṣafwaan, to get some more milk and food.
   (e) to help him to remember the proper way of entering a house.

4. When are the three times that children must knock on their parents' doors and why should they do so for each time?

5. (a) Mention three etiquettes for entering houses when visiting.

   (b) What are the two bad results which could occur if the proper method for entering houses is not followed?

6. What is Islaam's attitude toward peeping in houses without permission.

13. ḤADEETH FIVE: CHEATING

عَنْ أَبِى هُرَيْرَةَ أَنَّ رَسُوْلَ اللهِ ﷺ مَرَّ فِي السُّوْقِ عَلَى حُبْرَةِ طَعَامٍ ، فَأَدْخَلَ يَدَهُ فِيْهَا ، فَنَالَتْ أَصَابِعُهُ بَلَلًا ، فَقَالَ : «مَاهذَا يَاصَاحِبَ الطَّعَامِ ؟» قَالَ : يَارَسُوْلَ اللهِ أَصَابَتْهُ السَّمَاءُ ، قَالَ : «أَفَلَا جَعَلْتَهُ فَوْقَ الطَّعَامِ حَتَّى يَرَاهُ النَّاسُ ؟» ، وَقَالَ : «مَنْ غَشَّنَا فَلَيْسَ مِنَّا» رَوَاهُ مُسْلِمٌ وَالتِّرْمِذِيُّ وَأَبُو دَاود .

Abu Hurayrah reported that Allaah's Messenger (ﷺ) passed by a pile of food stuff and stuck his hand into it. When he found it wet, he asked its owner, "What is that?" The trader replied, "Rain fell on it, O Messenger of Allaah." The Prophet (ﷺ) then said, "Why didn't you put it on top so that the people could see it? Whoever cheats us is not of us."

Collected by Muslim, at-Tirmidhee and Abu Daawood[1]

The Narrator

Abu Hurayrah's biography can be found in *Ḥadeeth* number two.

The Collector

Muslim's biography can be found in *Ḥadeeth* number one, Abu Daawood's in *Ḥadeeth* number three and at-Tirmidhee's in *Ḥadeeth* number four.

GENERAL MEANING

One day when the Prophet (ﷺ) was in the market place, Allaah revealed to him that one of the traders was deceiving the people. So

---

[1] *Sahih Muslim* (English Trans.), vol. 1, p. 58, no. 183 and *Sunan Abu Dawud* (English Trans.), vol. 2, p. 982, no. 3445.

when he passed by a heap of wheat grain belonging to the trader, he stuck his hand into it and felt the wet grain in its center. He then questioned the trader who owned the grain about why he did this. The Prophet (ﷺ) questioned the trader, even though he knew before hand why the man had done it. This was in order to expose him and his bad practise to all the people in the market place. The Prophet (ﷺ) wanted to make him an example to all of the other traders. The owner of the wet grain explained that the grain had accidentally gotten wet the previous night due to rainfall. The Prophet (ﷺ) then scolded him, by telling him that he should let the people know exactly what he was selling and not try to cheat them. If goods are damaged the trader should inform the buyer of it, otherwise he is cheating. After that, the Prophet (ﷺ) turned to the other traders and told them that whoever cheats is not a true follower of Islaam. Such an individual is not a true Muslim, because he has forgotten that Allaah is watching him and that he will have to answer for what he has done on the day of Judgement. The Prophet (ﷺ) emphasized honesty in business dealings saying, *"Both parties in a sale can cancel it as long as they have not separated. If they are honest their sale will be blessed, but if they are dishonest the blessing will be removed."*[1]

Some students do not study properly, but manage to pass by either dishonestly carrying answers into the examination room or by looking at the examination papers of others. Such behaviour is totally un-Islamic. It is cheating no matter what name people might call it or what excuses might be given for it. Islaam is firmly opposed to cheating in any of its forms. Those who supply answers for cheaters often claim that they are not cheating, but helping those in need. "Friends must help each other" they say. But Allaah has forbidden helping others in sin. He said in the Qur'aan:

وَتَعَاوَنُوا۟ عَلَى ٱلْبِرِّ وَٱلتَّقْوَىٰ وَلَا تَعَاوَنُوا۟ عَلَى ٱلْإِثْمِ وَٱلْعُدْوَٰنِ

---

[1] Narrated by Ḥakeem ibn Hizaam and collected by Muslim *(Sahih Muslim* (English Trans.), vol. 3, pp. 804-5, no. 3661).

Help each other in righteousness and piety, but do not help each other in sin and aggression.

(Soorah al-Maa'idah (5):2)

On one occasion the Prophet (ﷺ) quoted a common motto among Arabs in pre-Islamic times, *"Help your brother whether he is doing wrong or wrong has been done to him."* So the people asked, "Messenger of Allaah, we can help him when he has been wronged but how can we help him when he is doing wrong?" The Prophet (ﷺ) replied, *"By preventing him."*[1] Consequently, the only way to help a friend who is cheating or wishes to cheat is to stop them from doing so. Otherwise, to help them commit a sin is in itself a sin. Even if one is not caught by the teacher, Allaah sees him and his sin has been recorded. Allaah may cause some misfortune to happen to him as punishment and a reminder in this life or He may leave it for punishment on the Day of Judgement. The cheater will not escape his sin for Allaah has said,

وَمَن يَعْمَلْ مِثْقَالَ ذَرَّةٍ شَرًّا يَرَهُ

"And whoever does an atom's weight of evil will face it."

(Soorah al-Zalzalah (99):8)

On the other hand the virtue of honesty is highly praised in Islaam. In fact, the Prophet Muhammad (ﷺ) was known as *al-Ameen* (The Honest) by his tribe, the Quraysh, even before he became a prophet. Allaah has also stated very clearly in the Qur'aan,

يَـٰٓأَيُّهَا ٱلَّذِينَ ءَامَنُوٓاْ أَوْفُواْ بِٱلْعُقُودِ

"Oh Believers, fulfill (your) obligations."

(Soorah al-Maa'idah (5):1)

Thus, the true Muslim has to be honest and reliable in his day-to-day

---

[1] Collected by al-Bukhaaree *(Sahih Bukhari* (Arabic-English), vol. 3, pp. 373-4, no. 624), at-Tirmidhee and Ahmad.

dealings with people otherwise he can not be considered to be a true Muslim.

Lessons

1. This *Hadeeth* teaches us that the leaders of Muslims should check up on the people from time to time, to make sure that they are dealing fairly with each other.

2. It also teaches us that, if someone is selling something which is defective or damaged, he should not hide the defects but should instead expose it so that the buyer can see exactly what he is buying.

3. This *Hadeeth* is clear proof that cheating is forbidden *(Haraam)* in Islaam and should be avoided at all costs.

4. It also informs us that a Muslim who cheats is not a true Muslim at all.

QUESTIONS

1. (a) What was Abu Hurayrah's real name?

   (b) Where was he born?

   (c) Who nicknamed him and why?

   (d) What was he most famous for?

2. In the *Hadeeth* on Cheating, the Prophet (ﷺ) knew that the grain merchant was cheating
   (a) when he stuck his hand into a pile of grain and found the center wet.
   (b) because he appeared nervous when the Prophet (ﷺ) came near him.
   (c) because the weight of the grain was more than normal.
   (d) when God informed him.
   (e) none of the above.

3. The Prophet (ﷺ) publicly scolded the trader because
   (a) he was a non-Muslim who was cheating Muslims.
   (b) the trader was well-known for his dishonesty.
   (c) the Prophet (ﷺ) wanted to make an example of him to the others.
   (d) he was very angry at him for trying to cheat him.
   (e) the trader was a Jew.

4. If one has damaged goods for sale one should
   (a) pretend that they are in working order or else no one will buy them.
   (b) not sell them, but instead either give them away or discard them.
   (c) inform those who wish to buy them of their defects.
   (d) sell them for a cheaper price.
   (e) allow the buyer to return them if he discovers the defects in time.

5. The Prophet (ﷺ) stated that cheaters were not true Muslims

(a) because all non-Muslims cheat.

(b) since Allaah said in the Qur'aan that cheaters are disbelievers.

(c) to inform the people present that the trader with the wet grain was a non-Muslim.

(d) because cheaters forget that   God sees them and will eventually judge them.

(e) as it is impossible for a true Muslim to even think of cheating anyone.

6. If someone asks us to help them cheat we should
    (a) help them only one time.
    (b) help them only if they are our close friends.
    (c) not help them unless the situation is very serious.
    (d) not help them and advise them not to do so.
    (e) help them but advise them that it is wrong.

7. Mention the good characteristic which the Prophet (ﷺ) is trying to teach us in this *Hadeeth*.

14. USOOL AL-FIQH: THE SOURCES OF ISLAMIC LAW

Islamic law is fundamentally based on the main two sources of divine revelation: the *Qur'aan* which represents the direct word of God to man, and the *Sunnah* which may be called the indirect word of God. Allaah has said in the Qur'aan concerning the statements of the Prophet Muhammad (ﷺ):

"He (Muhammad) does not speak from his desires. It is nothing but revelation sent down to him."

(Soorah an-Najm (53):3-4)

The laws contained in these two sources are primary laws which can not be changed at any time.

However, in the understanding and application of these laws, secondary sources have evolved. The most significant of them to this study of *Usool al-Fiqh* are *Ijmaa'*, a consensus of opinion, and *Qiyaas*, the deduction of rulings by comparison.

Method

If we want to know how we should govern a country, or how we should judge criminals, as well as settle disputes between people, or even how to run our families, we should first look in the Qur'aan, to see what Allaah has to say on it. If we do not find a sufficient answer in the Qur'aan, we then turn to the *Sunnah* to see what the Prophet (ﷺ) did or said related to the topic. If we can not find what we are looking for, we look to see what points of law the *Sahaabah* (Companions of the Prophet (ﷺ) agreed on. This area of agreement is called *Ijmaa'*. If, after that, we are still unable to find what we are looking for, we are then allowed to use our own reasoning to come to a decision. This decision should have some support from the Qur'aan, the *Sunnah* or *Ijmaa'*, and if it does, it is called *Qiyaas*.

1. THE QUR'AAN

The Qur'aan is the word of Allaah as revealed to His last Prophet, Muhammad (ﷺ), in Arabic rhyme, whose recitation is used in *Salaah* and other forms of worship, and whose smallest chapter is a miracle in itself.

Miracle of the Qur'aan

1. Allaah in the Qur'aan challenged the Arabs, as well as all of mankind, saying to them,

وَإِن كُنتُمْ فِى رَيْبٍ مِّمَّا نَزَّلْنَا عَلَىٰ عَبْدِنَا فَأْتُواْ بِسُورَةٍ مِّن مِّثْلِهِ

"If you are in doubt about that which We have revealed to Our servant, bring one *Soorah* (chapter) similar to it"

(Soorah al-Baqarah (2):23)

We all know that the smallest *Soorah* in the Qur'aan is *Soorah al-Kawthar* having only 3 short verses yet, the Arabs at the time when the Qur'aan was revealed were unable to make one like it.

2. The Qur'aan contains certain scientific facts which were unknown in those days. For example, Allaah says that the chest of the disbeliever becomes tight as if he were ascending upwards into the sky,

وَمَن يُرِدْ أَن يُضِلَّهُ يَجْعَلْ صَدْرَهُ ضَيِّقًا حَرَجًا كَأَنَّمَا يَصَّعَّدُ فِى ٱلسَّمَآءِ

"He whom He (Allaah) wills to leave astray, He makes his chest tight and compressed as if he were ascending up into the sky."

(Soorah al-An'aam (6):125)

It was only recently that man discovered that the higher up into the atmosphere he travels, the less oxygen is present. So if one goes up high enough, he will have difficulty breathing and his chest will feel as if it is tightening due to the lack of oxygen. Allaah also talks in the Qur'aan about the movement of the sun and the moon saying that,

وَهُوَ ٱلَّذِى خَلَقَ ٱلَّيْلَ وَٱلنَّهَارَ وَٱلشَّمْسَ وَٱلْقَمَرَ كُلٌّ فِى فَلَكٍ يَسْبَحُونَ

"It is He who created the night and day, the sun and the moon, all of them are floating in orbits."

(Soorah al-Anbiyaa (21):33)

Man only a few years ago found out that the moon travels around the earth in an orbit. As for the Sun, they now admit that it is moving within the Milky Way Galaxy which is itself moving in space also. But as of yet, they have not determined the exact pattern of its motion. Some feel it is in a straight line while others feel, it might be circular. There are countless other scientific facts mentioned in the Qur'aan which were totally unknown 1,400 years ago proving that it could only have come from the Creator.

3. Allaah also made the Qur'aan very easy to memorize. So easy, that millions and millions of Muslims have memorized it since its revelation. It is no smaller than the New Testament which Christians follow, yet no one has been known to have ever memorized the New Testament.

4. Allaah has protected the Qur'aan from any change at all. From the time it was revealed until now, it has remained the same. Allaah made a promise in the Qur'aan at the time of its revelation that He would protect it from change.

إِنَّا نَحْنُ نَزَّلْنَا ٱلذِّكْرَ وَإِنَّا لَهُ لَحَافِظُونَ

"Certainly it is We who revealed the Reminder (Qur'aan) and it is indeed We who will protect it."

(Soorah al-Ḥijr (15):9)

If all the other religious books in the world were destroyed, the only book which could be rewritten exactly as it was, is the Qur'aan.

Examples of Laws Derived from the Qur'aan

(a) Inheritance

If a person dies and leaves behind wealth for his children, it must be divided up amongst his heirs according to some system of rules. The Qur'aan provides certain basic laws for the division of inheritance among the relatives of the deceased. Allaah says:

يُوصِيكُمُ ٱللَّهُ فِى أَوْلَٰدِكُمْ لِلذَّكَرِ مِثْلُ حَظِّ ٱلْأُنثَيَيْنِ فَإِن كُنَّ نِسَآءً فَوْقَ ٱثْنَتَيْنِ فَلَهُنَّ ثُلُثَا مَا تَرَكَ وَإِن كَانَتْ وَٰحِدَةً فَلَهَا ٱلنِّصْفُ

"Allaah advises you concerning your children's (inheritance): the male should get a portion equal to that of two females. If there are only daughters, two or more should receive two-thirds of the inheritance and if only one her share is a half."

(Soorah an-Nisaa' (4):11)

(b) Theft

Similarly, if a person is caught stealing, the punishment for such a crime is mentioned in the Qur'aan. Allaah said:

وَٱلسَّارِقُ وَٱلسَّارِقَةُ فَٱقْطَعُوٓا۟ أَيْدِيَهُمَا جَزَآءًۢ بِمَا كَسَبَا نَكَٰلًا مِّنَ ٱللَّهِ وَٱللَّهُ عَزِيزٌ حَكِيمٌ

"Cut off the hands of the male and female thief as a punishment by example from Allaah, for their crime."

(Soorah al-Maa'idah (5):38)

II. SUNNAH

The *Sunnah* represents the record of the true sayings, actions and approvals of the Prophet (ﷺ) which were related by his *Sahaabah* (companions) to the next generation of Muslims and collected in books by those scholars who came after them. After the Prophet (ﷺ) passed away, the companions were left to run the Islamic state based on the principles found in the Qur'aan and whatever else the Prophet (ﷺ) had taught them. If a problem arose which could not be solved by using the Qur'aan alone, the Khaleefah [1] would ask among the companions if anyone had heard the Prophet (ﷺ) say anything concerning it. Usually someone would get up and say I heard the Prophet (ﷺ) say so and so, or I saw him do this or that. In this way the sayings and actions of the Prophet (ﷺ) became common knowledge to many. As the borders of the Islamic state expanded and large numbers of people accepted Islaam, many would travel miles to come and study under the Sahaabah in order to learn Islaam. The Sahaabah would tell them what they heard the Prophet (ﷺ) say, or show them what they saw the Prophet (ﷺ) do. In this way the sayings and actions of the Prophet (ﷺ) were handed down to the next generation of Muslims referred to as the Taabi'oon. It was during the era of the Taabi'oon that Hadeeths began to be recorded in writing on a fairly large scale, but it was really in the following generation known as the Atbaa' at-Taabi'een and the generation following them that Hadeeth were organized according to subject matter and put in one of the six major books of Hadeeths called the Sihaah as-Sittah. [2]

Examples of Laws Derived from the Sunnah

(a) Inheritance

The division of inheritance for close family members is clearly explained in the Qur'aan. But, the leaving of wealth for non-Muslim relatives is not mentioned in the Qur'aan. In the Sunnah we find that the Prophet (ﷺ) said, *"A Muslim may not inherit from a non-Muslim, nor may a non-Muslim inherit from a Muslim."* [3]

(b) Theft

The minimum amount for which a thief's hand may be cut off and how much of the hand is to be cut off can only be found in the Sunnah.

---

[1] Caliph - Head of the Islamic State.

[2] Literally, "the Authentic Six". They are: the two Saheehs al-Bukhaaree and Muslim, and the four Sunans of Abu Daawood, at-Tirmidhee, an-Nasaa'ee and Ibn Maajah.

[3] Reported by Usaamah ibn Zayd and collected by Muslim (Sahih Muslim (English Trans.), vol. 3, p. 852, no. 3928).

'Aa'ishah reported that Allaah's Messenger (ﷺ) said, *"The hand of a thief can only be cut off for (the value of) a quarter of a dinar and upwards."*[1]

III. IJMAA'

Ijmaa' is the joint agreement of the *Sahaabah* on a point of Islamic Law not found in either the Qur'aan or the *Sunnah,* but based on one of them (not disagreeing with what is in them). When certain problems arose after the death of the Prophet (ﷺ), the *Sahabaah* used to gather together to try and solve them. They would go over the Qur'aan to see if Allaah had something specific to say on the subject, and if they found nothing, the *Khaleefah* (Muslim leader) would ask if anyone had heard the Prophet (ﷺ) say anything concerning it. If they still did not find the answer, the *Khaleefah* would then give his opinion and so would others, if they thought that their ideas were better. The various opinions would then be discussed until they agreed on the best one and then they would make it into a law for all the Muslims.

In this way the laws of Islaam could be molded to fit all times and all circumstances. The new laws which were made by *Ijmaa'* were not basic laws, as all the basic laws had already been set down by Allaah in the Qur'aan and by the Prophet (ﷺ) in his *Sunnah.* These laws were secondary laws which could vary according to various situations.

Examples of Laws Derived by Ijmaa'

(a) Collection of the Qur'aan

The Qur'aan was revealed to the Prophet (ﷺ) in sections over a period of 23 years. Whenever a verse was revealed the Prophet (ﷺ) had some of his companions write it down on whatever was available, and many memorized it when the Prophet (ﷺ) recited it in *Salaah.* The Prophet (ﷺ) did not have the written sections of the Qur'aan gathered together in one book during his life time. After the Prophet's death, the various sections of the Qur'aan, which were writ-

---

[1] *Sahih Muslim* (English Trans.), vol. 3, p. 907, no. 4179.

ten down on tree barks, animal skins and bones, remained in the possession of the *Ṣahaabah*. Most of them had also memorized large portions of the Qur'aan during the Prophet's (ﷺ) lifetime, but there were only a few who had memorized the whole Qur'aan.

During the reign of the first Caliph Abu Bakr, the *Ṣahaabah* decided by *Ijmaa'* that they should gather all the pieces of the Qur'aan together into one complete book. The job was given to Zayd ibn Thaabit since he was one of the Prophet's (ﷺ) scribes and he had memorized all of it and had recited it back to the Prophet (ﷺ) a number of times. Zayd gathered all that had been written and compared it with what he and others had memorized, then wrote it down in one book, which he turned over to the Caliph.

(b) The Adhaans of Jumu'ah

During the time of the Prophet (ﷺ) there was only one *Adhaan* for the *Salaah* of *Jumu'ah* (Friday congregational prayer) and it was made when the Prophet (ﷺ) entered the *Masjid* (Mosque) and said, *"Salaam 'alaykum"*. During the reign of the first and second Caliphs the *Adhaan* remained as it was, but during the reign of the third Caliph, 'Uthmaan ibn 'Affaan, another *Adhaan* was added. The city of Madeenah had become large and so had its market place, so much so, that the *Adhaan* of *Jumu'ah* was drowned out by the noise of the traders and their customers. Realizing this, Caliph 'Uthmaan suggested to the other *Ṣahaabah* that another *Adhaan* be called before the main *Adhaan,* and that it be done in the middle of the market. They all agreed by *Ijmaa'*, and thus another *Adhaan* was added.

IV. QIYAAS [1]

Qiyaas is the deduction of Islamic Laws not found in the Qur'aan, the *Sunnah* or *Ijmaa'*, but based on laws found in one of them. If a problem arises which none of the first three sources addressed directly, we then try to find a law in any one of them which had a similar cause, and

---

[1] A conclusion from observation.

classify the problem in a similar manner.

Examples of Laws Derived by Qiyaas

(a) Drugs

For example, drugs like marijuana and cocaine (crack) were not around in the Prophet's (囊) time nor in the time of the *Sahaabah*, so nothing direct was said concerning them. However, the Prophet (囊) had said: *"Every intoxicant is* **Khamr,**[1] *so every intoxicant is Haraam."*[2] When we observe those who smoke or inject marijuana, cocaine and similar drugs, we notice that they lose some if not all of their senses, they become high (intoxicated). Therefore, we can conclude that marijuana and coke are forms of *Khamr*, and therefore they are *Haraam*. As for those who say that they only take a little bit and it does not make them intoxicated, the Prophet (囊) also said, *"Whatever intoxicates in large amounts is* **Haraam** *in small amounts."*[3]

(b) Smoking

When cigarettes and tobacco first reached the Ottoman Muslim empire in the 17th century most scholars ruled by *Qiyaas* that it was *Makrooh* (disliked), because the only known ill effects at that time was "smoker's breath", which was offensive. This ruling was based on an authentic *Hadeeth* in which the Prophet (囊) had said, *"Whoever eats any of this offensive plant (garlic) should not come to the mosque." The people said, "It has been forbidden! It has been forbidden!" When this reached the Prophet (囊), he said, "O people, I can not forbid what Allaah has made lawful, but it is a plant whose odour I dis-*

---

[1] *Khamr* is literally an alcoholic drink made from fermented grape juice.

[2] Reported by Ibn 'Umar and collected by al-Bukhaaree and Muslim *(Sahih Muslim* (English Trans.), vol. 3, pp. 1108-9, no. 4966), Abu Daawood *(Sunan Abu Dawud* (English Trans.), vol. 3, p. 1043, no. 3671) and at-Tirmidhee.

[3] Reported by Jaabir ibn 'Abdillaah and collected by Ibn Maajah and Abu Daawood *(Sunan Abu Dawud* (English Trans.), vol. 3, pp. 1043-4, no. 3673) and rated *Saheeh* in *Saheeh Sunan Abee Daawood*, vol. 2, p. 702, no. 3128.

like."[1] On another occasion he included onions and leek as also offensive.[2] However, in our times the medical profession has now stated that smoking causes cancer alongwith a number of other illnesses. Since, in most cases cancer causes death, it can now be said that smoking kills. So, a number of scholars now rule by *Qiyaas* that smoking is *Haraam,* because one who does so is, in fact, committing suicide and Allaah has said:

$$وَلَا نَقْتُلُوٓاْ أَنفُسَكُمْ إِنَّ ٱللَّهَ كَانَ بِكُمْ رَحِيمًا$$

"And do not kill yourselves, for Allaah is indeed merciful to you."

(Soorah an-Nisaa' (4):29)

$$وَلَا تُلْقُواْ بِأَيْدِيكُمْ إِلَى ٱلتَّهْلُكَةِ$$

"...and do not throw yourselves into destruction with your own hands."

(Soorah al-Baqarah (2):195)

The Prophet (ﷺ) also said: *"Whoever kills himself with a knife will be in Hell forever stabbing himself in his stomach. Whoever drinks poison and kills himself will drink it eternally in the Hell fire. And whoever kills himself by falling off a mountain will forever fall in the fire of Hell."*[3]

According to Islamic law, it makes no difference whether someone kills himself by taking small amounts of poison over a long period of time or a large enough amount all at once, It is *Haraam* to take any substance which is known to be harmful.

---

[1] Reported by Abu Sa'eed and collected by Muslim *(Sahih Muslim* (English Trans.), vol. 1, p. 280, no. 1149).

[2] Reported by Jaabir ibn 'Abdillaah and collected by Muslim *(Sahih Muslim* (English Trans.), vol. 1, p. 280, no. 1147).

[3] Reported by Abu Hurayrah and collected by Muslim *(Sahih Muslim* (English Trans.), vol. 1, p. 62, no. 199).

Significance

By using the principle of *Qiyaas* the basic laws of Islaam can be applied at anytime and in any place. New rulings can be made for any new circumstances, based on their similarities with the basic laws of the Qur'aan and the *Sunnah*. In this way, the divine laws revealed in the Qur'aan and *Sunnah* remain unchanged without becoming out-dated. It can not be successfully argued that Islamic law can not be applied in the 20th century because it is 1,400 years old. The funda-mental laws of Islaam were made by God who created man and knows what is best for him under all circumstances. There are certain basic characteristics of man which do not change with time or location. It is these areas which the basic laws of Islaam address. As for the chang-ing aspects of human life, the Qur'aan and *Sunnah* provide basic prin-ciples which may be applied by *Qiyaas* whenever the need arises. Thus, Islamic law is suitable for mankind in all eras wherever he may be, whether on earth or on the planets or on a distant star.

QUESTIONS

1. The primary sources of Islamic law are
   (a) the Qur'aan, the Sunnah, *Ijmaa'* and *Qiyaas*.
   (b) the Qur'aan, the Sunnah and *Ijmaa'*.
   (c) the Qur'aan and the Sunnah.
   (d) *Ijmaa'* and *Qiyaas*.
   (e) The Qur'aan and *Qiyaas*.

2. They are considered primary sources of Islamic law
   (a) their laws were revealed by Allaah.
   (b) their laws were agreed upon by all the *Sahaabah*.
   (c) their laws were deduced from the Qur'aan.
   (d) Allaah called them that in the Qur'aan.
   (e) the secondary sources are based on divine revelation.

3. Briefly explain how we should use the four main sources of Islamic law according to their order of importance.

4. Briefly explain in your own words three miracles of Qur'aan.

5. The Sunnah may be properly defined as
   (a) the actions of the Prophet (ﷺ) which were related by Muslims and collected in books by the *Sahaabah*.
   (b) the sayings, actions and approvals of the *Sahaabah* related by the Prophet (ﷺ) to the next generation of Muslims who recorded them in books.
   (c) the true sayings of the Prophet's companions on a point of Islamic law not found in the Qur'aan or the *Ijmaa'*.
   (d) the sayings of the Prophet (ﷺ) recorded in the Qur'aan and related by his *Sahaabah*.
   (e) a record of the true sayings, actions and approvals of the Prophet (ﷺ) related by his companions to the next generation of Muslims and collected in books by scholars who came after them.

6. The Sunnah of the Prophet (ﷺ) became common knowledge among the early Muslims.

(a) because it was written down in one book by the Caliph when many *Sahaabah* died during the wars of apostasy and the Sunnah was nearly lost.

(b) because after the Prophet's ( ) death when new problems arose, the *Sahaabah* would agree on a solution and make it a law.

(c) because after the Prophet's ( ) death the Caliph would gather the *Sahaabah* whenever a problem arose and ask if they heard anything from the Prophet ( ) about it.

(d) when they collected the Qur'aan into one book after the death of the Prophet ( ).

(e) in order to find solutions for problems which arose during the time of the Prophet ( ).

7. (a) Briefly explain in your own words how *Ijmaa'* came about.

(b) Were the new laws which came from *Ijmaa'* basic laws?

(c) Give two examples of *Ijmaa'*.

8. (a) How is *Qiyaas* used?

(b) Give an example of *Qiyaas*.

(c) Briefly explain the importance of *Qiyaas* to the application of Islamic law.

15. FIQH: ṬAHAARAH

Ṭahaarah literally means "purity," but Islamically it refers to a state of cleanliness which a Muslim must be in to perform certain acts of worship. Although the various acts of *Ṭahaarah* may make us physically clean, the real purpose behind *Ṭahaarah* is spiritual cleanliness. By entering into a state of *Ṭahaarah*, one prepares oneself spiritually to worship Allaah.

ACTS WHICH BREAK ṬAHAARAH

The following are the acts which break one's state of purity and require *Wuḍoo*. As a group they are called *al-Ḥadath al-Aṣghar* (Minor Defilement).

1. Passing Wind.

'Abbaad ibn Tameem said, *"My uncle asked Allaah's Messenger (ﷺ) about a person who imagined that he passed wind during his Ṣalaah (prayer). Allaah's Messenger (ﷺ) replied, "He should not leave his prayer unless he hears a sound or smells something."*[1]

2. Passing Urine.

3. Passing Feces.

In the Qur'aan Allaah says:

أَوْ جَاءَ أَحَدٌ مِّنكُم مِّنَ ٱلْغَآئِطِ

"...or if one of you comes from relieving himself."
(Soorah an-Nisaa' (4):43)

4. Deep Sleep.

Ṣafwaan ibn 'Assaal said, *"The Prophet (ﷺ) told us that when we are on a journey we need not remove our leather socks for three days*

---

[1] Collected by al-Bukhaaree *(Sahih Al-Bukhari* (Arabic-English), vol. 1, p. 102, no. 139) and Muslim *(Sahih Muslim* (English Trans.), vol. 1, p. 199, no. 702).

and their nights (to make **Wuḍoo**) because of passing feces, urine or sleep."[1]

'Alee ibn Abee Ṭaalib also reported that the Prophet (ﷺ) said, *"The eye is the drawstring of the anus, so whoever sleeps should make* **Wuḍoo.**"[2]

In the case where one sleeps sitting upright deep sleep does not break the state of *Tahaarah*. Anas said, *"The Prophet's companions used to wait for the night prayer until their heads would nod, then get up and perform* **Ṣalaah** *without making* **Wuḍoo.**"[3]

5. Touching The Privates.

Busrah bint Ṣafwaan narrated that the Prophet (ﷺ) said, *"Whoever touches his privates can not make* **Ṣalaah** *until he does* **Wuḍoo.**"[4] This is the case when the touching occurs inside one's clothes and not from the outside, as Abu Hurayrah reported that he heard the Prophet (ﷺ) say, *"Whoever touches his privates with his hand without any covering between them must make* **Wuḍoo.**"[5]

---

[1] Collected by Aḥmad, an-Nasaa'ee and at-Tirmidhee and rated authentic *(Hasan)* by al-Albaanee in *Irwaa al-Ghaleel*, vol. 1, p. 140, no. 104.

[2] Collected by Abu Daawood *(Sunan Abu Dawud* (English Trans.), vol. 1, p. 50, no. 203), Ibn Maajah and ad-Daaraqutnee and rated authentic *(Hasan)* in *Irwaa al-Ghaleel*, vol. 1, p. 148, no. 113.

[3] Collected by Muslim, *(Sahih Muslim* (English Trans.), vol. 1, p. 205, no. 733), at-Tirmidhee and Abu Daawood, *(Sunan Abu Dawud* (English Trans.), vol. 1, p. 49, no. 200).

[4] Collected by at-Tirmidhee, Abu Daawood *(Sunan Abu Dawud* (English Trans.), vol. 1, pp. 43-4, no. 181), an-Nasaa'ee, Ibn Maajah, Aḥmad and Maalik *(Muwatta Imam Malik,* (English Trans.), pp. 19-20, no. 86), and rated *Ṣaheeḥ* in *Irwaa al-Ghaleel*, vol. 1, p. 150, no. 116.

[5] Reported by Abu Hurayrah and collected by Aḥmad, al-Ḥaakim, al-Bayhaqee, ad-Daaraqutnee and Ibn Ḥibbaan, and rated *Ṣaheeḥ* by al-Albaanee in *Ṣaheeḥ al-Jaami' aṣ-Ṣagheer*, vol. 1, p. 126, no. 326.

6. Eating Camel's Meat.

Jaabir ibn Samurah said, *"A man asked the Prophet (ﷺ), 'Should I make **Wuḍoo** after eating mutton?' He replied, 'If you wish.' 'He then asked, 'Should I make **Wuḍoo** after eating camel meat?' He replied, 'Yes!' "[1]*

Being in a state of *Tahaarah* is a condition which must be fulfilled before Allaah will accept our *Salaah*. The Prophet Muhammad (ﷺ) said, *"**Salaah** is not accepted from one who breaks his state of **Tahaarah** until he makes **Wuḍoo**."[2]* Therefore if any of the above mentioned acts take place to anyone of us,[3] we are forbidden from mak-

---

[1] Collected by Muslim *(Sahih Muslim* (English Trans.), vol. 1, p. 198, no. 700).

[2] Collected by al-Bukhaaree *(Sahih Al-Bukhari* (Arabic-English), vol. 1, p. 101, no. 137) and Muslim *(Sahih Muslim* (English Trans.), vol. 1, p. 149, no. 435).

[3] **Note Concerning Vomiting and Blood:** The *Hadeeth* attributed to 'Aa'eshah that the Prophet (ﷺ) said, *"Whoever is afflicted by Qay, Ru'aaf or Qals (different forms of vomiting) should leave (the Salaah), make Wuḍoo, then continue where he left off without speaking during it,"* is inaccurate *(Ḍa'eef)*. See al-Albaanee's, *Ḍa'eef al-Jaami' as-Sagheer*, vol. 5, p. 167, no. 5434. Therefore, it can not be used as proof that vomiting breaks *Wuḍoo*. The only authentic narration on vomiting is that of Abud-Dardaa in which he stated that the Prophet (ﷺ) vomited then made *Wuḍoo* (collected by Aḥmad and at-Tirmidhee and rated *Saheeh* in *Irwaa al-Ghaleel*, vol. 1, p. 147, no. 111). However, this tradition only indicates the Prophet's (ﷺ) *Sunnah*. It does not indicate that *Wuḍoo* is necessary *(Waajib)* in the case of vomiting.

In the case of blood (other than menses) from a wound, there are no authentic traditions wherein *Wuḍoo* is required. The *"Hadeeth"* of Tameem ad-Daaree quoting the Prophet (ﷺ) as saying, *"Wuḍoo should be done in every case of blood which flows."* (collected by ad-Daaraqutnee) is extremely weak. (See al-Albaanee's edition of *Mishkaah al-Maṣaabeeḥ*, vol. 1, p. 108, no. 333). Imaam al-Bukhaaree quoted Jaabir ibn 'Abdillaah as saying, "The Prophet (ﷺ) was in the battle of Dhaat ar-Ruqaa' and a person who was shot with an arrow bled profusely, but he bowed and prostrated continuing his prayer." He also quoted the Prophet's grandson al-Ḥasan as saying, "The Muslims used to pray despite their wounds," and stated that Ibn 'Umar squeezed one of his pimples and blood came out, but he did not repeat his *Wuḍoo. (Sahih Al-Bukhari*, (Arabic-English), vol. 1, p. 121, no. 35).

ing *Salaah* until we regain or attain a proper state of *Tahaarah*. The state of *Tahaarah* may be gained by making *Wudoo* or *Ghusl* (a complete bath) if water is available, and by *Tayammum* (purification by dust) if water is not present.

WUDOO

The law concerning *Tahaarah* and *Salaah* can be found in the Qur'aan as follows:

يَـٰٓأَيُّهَا ٱلَّذِينَ ءَامَنُوٓاْ إِذَا قُمْتُمْ إِلَى ٱلصَّلَوٰةِ فَٱغْسِلُواْ وُجُوهَكُمْ وَأَيْدِ
يَكُمْ إِلَى ٱلْمَرَافِقِ وَٱمْسَحُواْ بِرُءُوسِكُمْ وَأَرْجُلَكُمْ إِلَى ٱلْكَعْبَيْنِ

"Oh believers if you get up to make *Salaah*, you should wash your faces and hands up to your elbows. Then you should wipe your heads and wash your feet up to your ankles."

(Soorah al-Maa'idah (5):6)

This is a general description of the form of purification known as *Wudoo*. The *Sunnah* of the Prophet (ﷺ) gives us the details as follows:

Neeyah

The Prophet Muhammad (ﷺ) was reported to have said, *"Surely deeds (are judged) by their intentions, and every man gets (according to) his intentions."*[1] From this *Hadeeth* we can see that any good deed which is not done with the correct intention will not be counted in our favor on the Day of Judgement. Therefore, it is very important that we make the pleasure and remembrance of God our intention for doing any acts of worship. If care is not taken, acts of worship may be done only to please parents, teachers or to show off to our friends. Religious acts done with such intentions are considered a form of hidden *Shirk*.

---

[1] Reported by 'Umar and collected by al-Bukhaaree *(Sahih Al-Bukhari* (Arabic-English), vol. 1, p. 1, no. 1) and Muslim.

The Messenger of Allaah (ﷺ) was reported as saying, *"The Salaah of one without **Wudoo** is not valid and the **Wudoo** of one without the mention of Allaah's name is not valid."*[1] Thus, we should begin this act of worship with the mention of Allaah's name in order to gain all of the blessings contained in it.

Siwaak

It is recommended that we brush our teeth before or after *Wudoo* if we are going to make *Salaah* afterwards.

Abu Hurayrah reported that Allaah's Messenger (ﷺ) said, *"Were it not that I might over-burden the believers, I would have ordered them to use the **Siwaak** (tooth-stick) at the time of every **Salaah**."*[2] The main purpose of this is to keep our breath fresh so that we do not offend those praying beside us. It is also better for our teeth.

Wudoo

Humraan reported that 'Uthmaan called for water for *Wudoo* and he washed his hands to his wrists, then he put a handful of water with his right hand into his mouth, gargled with it and spat it out. He did this three times. Then he inhaled water into his nostrils from his right hand and exhaled it with the help of his left hand. He also did this three times. He then filled both his hands with water and washed his face three times. Then he washed his right arm up to his elbow three times and his left arm likewise. He then wet his hands and wiped them on his head once. Then he washed his right foot up to the ankle three times and likewise his left. He then said, "I saw Allaah's Messenger (ﷺ) perform *Wudoo* like this *Wudoo* of mine."[3]

---

[1] Reported by Abu Hurayrah and collected by Abu Daawood *(Sunan Abu Dawud* (English Trans.), vol. 1, p. 26, no. 26), no. 101), at-Tirmidhee and Ibn Maajah, and rated *Saheeh* in *Saheeh Sunan Abee Daawood,* vol. 1, p. 21, no. 92.

[2] Collected by Abu Daawood *(Sunan Abu Dawud* (English Trans.), vol. 1, p. 11, no. 46) and rated *Saheeh* in *Saheeh Sunan Abee Daawood,* vol. 1, pp. 11-12, no. 37.

[3] Collected by al-Bukhaaree *(Sahih Al-Bukhari* (Arabic-English) vol. 1, p. 113, no. 161 and p. 115, no. 165), Muslim *(Sahih Muslim* (English Trans.), vol. 1, p. 149, no. 436) and Abu Daawood *(Sunan Abu Dawud* (English Trans.), vol. 1, p. 28, no. 106).

Gargling and Inhaling

'Abdullaah ibn Zayd said, *"He (the Prophet* ﷺ *) gargled and inhaled water from one palm, doing that three times."*[1]

Wiping the Head

The whole head may be wiped with water left on the hands from washing or with fresh water. In describing the Prophet's (ﷺ) *Wudoo* some companions said,

"He wiped his head with fresh water, not the water left on his hands from washing them,"[2] and at other times, *"The Prophet (ﷺ) wiped his head with water left over from his hands."*[3]

Ar-Rubayyi' bint Mu'awwidh reported that she saw Allaah's Messenger (ﷺ) performing *Wudoo* and he wiped the whole of his head from the front to back including the sides without disturbing his hair.[4] However al-Miqdaam ibn Ma'deekarib also said, *"I saw Allaah's Messenger (ﷺ) perform **Wudoo** and when he reached the wiping of his head, he put his palms on the front of his head, moved them back to the beginning of his neck and back to where he started from."*[5]

---

[1] Collected by Muslim *(Sahih Muslim* (English Trans.), vol. 1, p. 152, no. 453 and Abu Daawood *(Sunan Abu Dawud* (English Trans.), vol. 1, p. 30, no. 119).

[2] Reported by 'Abdullaah ibn Zayd and collected by Muslim *(Sahih Muslim* (English Trans.), vol. 1, p. 153, no. 457 and Abu Daawood *(Sunan Abu Dawud* (English Trans.), vol. 1, p. 30-1, no. 120) and rated *Saheeh* in *Saheeh Sunan Abee Daawood,* vol. 1, p. 26, no. 111.

[3] Reported by ar-Rubbayyi' bint Mu'awwidh and collected by Abu Daawood *(Sunan Abu Dawud* (English Trans.), vol. 1, p. 31, no. 130) rated authentic *(Hasan)* in *Saheeh Sunan Abee Daawood,* vol. 1, p. 27, no. 120).

[4] Collected by Abu Daawood *(Sunan Abu Dawud* (English Trans.), vol. 1, p. 31, no. 128) and rated *Saheeh* in *Saheeh Sunan Abee Daawood,* vol. 1, p. 27, no. 118.

[5] Collected by Abu Daawood *(Sunan Abu Dawud* (English Trans.), vol. 1, p. 31, no. 122) and rated *Saheeh* in *Saheeh Sunan Abee Daawood* vol. 1, p. 26, no. 113.

Though most companions stated that the Prophet (ﷺ) only wiped his head once or twice as previously mentioned, Shaqeeq ibn Salamah reported that he did see 'Uthmaan ibn 'Affaan on one occasion wash his arms three times and wipe his head three times, then say, "I saw Allaah's Messenger (ﷺ) do it this way."[1]

The Ears

The ears should be properly wiped, inside and out.

Al-Miqdaam reported, *"Water for **Wuḍoo** was brought to Allaah's Messenger and he made **Wuḍoo** by washing his hands to the wrists thrice, gargling and inhaling water thrice, washing his face thrice and his arms thrice and wiping his head and his ears, outside and inside."*[2]

The thumb is used to wipe the back of the ear and the index finger is used for the inside.[3]

The Beard

Anas ibn Maalik said, *"Whenever Allaah's Messenger (ﷺ) made* **Wuḍoo,** *he would put a handful of water under his chin and pass his fingers through his beard, and say "This is how my Lord, most Great and Glorious, has commanded me."*[4]

Number of Times

The various parts of the body may be washed once, twice or thrice.

---

[1] Collected by Abu Daawood *(Sunan Abu Dawud* (English Trans.), vol. 1, p. 29, no. 110) and rated *Saheeh* by al-Albaanee in *Saheeh Sunan Abee Daawood*, vol. 1, p. 23, no. 101.

[2] Collected by Abu Daawood *(Sunan Abu Dawud* (English Trans.), vol. 1, p. 31, no. 121) and rated *Saheeh* in *Saheeh Sunan Abee Daawood*, vol. 1, p. 26, no. 112.

[3] For this description see 'Amr ibn Shu'ayb's *Hadeeth* on the following page under the heading **"Number of Times".**

[4] Collected by Abu Daawood *(Sunan Abu Dawud* (English Trans.), vol. 1, p. 35, no. 145) and rated *Saheeh* in *Saheeh Sunan Abee Daawood*, vol. 1, p. 30, no. 132.

However, three times is the maximum unless one discovers a dry area remaining.

Ibn 'Abbaas said, *"The Prophet (ﷺ) made **Wudoo** by washing the body parts* once."[1] 'Abdullaah ibn Zayd also said, *"The Prophet (ﷺ) made Wudoo by washing the body parts twice."*[2]

'Amr ibn Shu'ayb quoting his father on the authority of his grand-father, said, *"A man came to the Prophet (ﷺ) and asked him, 'Oh Messenger of Allaah, how should **Wudoo** be made?' He (the Prophet) called for a vessel of water and washed his hands upto his wrists thrice, his face thrice and his forearms twice. He then wiped his head, and inserted his index fingers into his ear and wiped the outer part with his thumbs and the inner part with his index fingers. Then he washed his feet three times and said, "This is how **Wudoo** is to be done. If anyone does more he has done wrong."*[3]

The Toes

Care should be taken to wash between the toes when washing the feet, as water may not get there otherwise.

Al-Mustawrid ibn Shiddaad said, *"I saw the Messenger of Allaah*

---

[1] Collected by al-Bukhaaree *Sahih Al-Bukhari* (Arabic-English), vol. 1, p. 112, no. 159) and Abu Daawood *(Sunan Abu Dawud* (English Trans.), vol. 1, p. 33, no. 138).

[2] Collected by al-Bukhaaree *Sahih Al-Bukhari* (Arabic-English), vol. 1, p. 112, no. 160) and Abu Daawood *(Sunan Abu Dawud* (English Trans.), vol. 1, p. 33, no. 136) from Abu Hurayrah.

[3] Collected by Abu Daawood *(Sunan Abu Dawud* (English Trans.), vol. 1, p. 32-3, no. 135, an-Nasaa'ee, Ibn Maajah and Ahmad, and rated *Saheeh* by al-Albaanee in *Saheeh Sunan Abee Daawood*, vol. 1, p. 28, no. 123 with the deletion of the words "or less".

Note concerning Wiping the Neck:
There are no authentic or unauthentic narrations in the major books of *Hadeeths* to support this wide spread practise. It has therefore been classified as a *Bid'ah* (a prohibited innovation in the religion).

(ﷺ) *rubbing between his toes with his little finger when he made* **Wuḍoo.**"[1]

Dry Spots

Wuḍoo should be done slowly and carefully to ensure that all of the parts to be washed are properly done.

'Abdillaah ibn 'Amr said, *"While we were returning from Makkah to Madeenah with Allaah's Messenger (ﷺ) we came across some water and some people hurriedly made* **Wuḍoo** *for the afternoon prayer (*'**Asr**). *When we reached them, their heels were dry as no water had touched them. The Prophet (ﷺ) said, "Woe to (dry) heels because of the Hellfire. Make your* **Wuḍoo** *thoroughly' "*[2]

Jaabir reported from 'Umar ibn al-Khaṭṭaab that a person performed *Wuḍoo* and left a small part equal to the size of a fingernail (unwashed) on his foot. Allaah's Messenger (ﷺ) saw it and said, *"Go back and make your* **Wuḍoo** *properly."*[3]

Du'aa

On completion of *Wuḍoo* the Prophet (ﷺ) used to say the following:

أَشْهَدُ أَنْ لَا إِلٰهَ الَّا الله وَحْدَهُ لَا شَرِيْكَ لَهُ وَأَشْهَدُ اَنَّ مُحَمَّداً عَبْدُهُ وَرَسُولُه

Ash-haduallaa elaaha illallaahu waḥdahoo laa shareeka lah, wa ash-hadu anna Muḥammadan 'abduhoo wa rasooluḥ

(I bear witness that there is no god but Allaah alone, without any partner, and I bear witness that Muḥammad is His servant and messenger).

---

[1] Collected by Abu Daawood *(Sunan Abu Dawud* (English Trans.), vol. 1, p. 36, no. 148) and rated *Saheeh* in *Saheeh Sunan Abee Daawood,* vol. 1, p. 30, no. 134).

[2] Collected by Muslim *(Sahih Muslim* (English Trans.), vol. 1, p. 154, no. 468).

[3] Collected by Muslim *(Sahih Muslim* (English Trans.), vol. 1, p. 155, no. 474) and Abu Daawood *(Sunan Abu Dawud* (English Trans.), vol. 1, p. 42, no. 173). The words "on his foot" is found in Abu Daawood's narration which is *Saheeh.*

The Prophet (ﷺ) also said that for whoever does the same, the eight gates of paradise will be opened and he may enter by any one he wishes.[1]

In another narration of this *Hadeeth* the Prophet (ﷺ) was reported to have added:

اللَّهُمَّ اجْعَلْنِى مِنَ التَّوَّابِيْنَ وَاجْعَلْنِى مِنَ الْمُتَطَهِّرِينَ

"Allaahummaj-'alnee minat-Tawwaabeena waj-'alnee minal-mutaṭah-hireen.
(Oh Allaah, make me among the constantly repentant and among those who are purified)

This *Du'aa* (prayer) reminds us of our faith and that the performance of *Wudoo* is basically for the rememberance of Allaah. In the *Du'aa* we are also taught to ask Allaah's forgiveness for our errors and that He purify us of our sins. So, when *Wudoo* is done properly for Allaah's sake, it can remove some of our bad deeds. Abu Hurayrah reported that Allaah's messenger (ﷺ) said, "*When a servant (of God) washes his face, every sinful thing he saw and thought about will be washed away with the last drop of water; when he washes his hands, every sin they did will be washed off from his hands with the last drop of water; and when he washes his feet, every sin towards which his feet have walked will be washed away with the last drop of water. So that he comes out pure from all sin.*"[2] As such, *Wudoo* should be done slowly and carefully and not in a race to see who can finish first.

GHUSL (COMPLETE BATH)

The Prophet Muhammad (ﷺ) strongly recommended Muslims to take a complete Islamic bath *(Ghusl)* on Fridays. When a person

---

[1] Reported by 'Umar and collected by Muslim *(Sahih Muslim* (English Trans.), vol. 1, p. 152, no. 451) and Abu Daawood *(Sunan Abu Dawud* (English Trans.), vol. 1, p. 41, no. 169).

[2] Collected by at-Tirmidhee and Ibn Maajah and rated *Saheeh* by al-Albaanee in *Saheeh Sunan at-Tirmidhee*, vol. 1, p. 18, no. 48.

newly converts to Islaam, the Prophet (ﷺ) also advised them to take a *Ghusl*. Qays ibn 'Aasim said, *"I came to the Prophet (ﷺ) in order to accept Islaam and he told me to take a **Ghusl** with water and **Sidr** (Lote-tree leaves)."*[1] Women are also required to purify themselves by *Ghusl* in order to start praying after their menses has ended.[2]

'Aa'eshah reported that when the Prophet (ﷺ) wanted to make *Ghusl* he used to first wash his hands then wash his private parts with his left hand. He would then make *Wudoo* like his *Wudoo* for *Salaah*. Then he would pour water on his head three times and rub it with his fingers into the roots of his hair. Following that he would pour water over the whole of his body[3] and he would sometimes move aside and wash his feet again.[4]

'Ubayd ibn 'Umayr reported that when 'Aa'eshah was informed that 'Abdullaah ibn 'Amr was ordering the women to undo their braids, she said, "It is strange that Ibn 'Amr is ordering women to undo their braids while taking *Ghusl*. Why doesn't he order them to shave their head (as it would be easier)? The Messenger of Allaah (ﷺ) and I made *Ghusl* from the same container and I only poured three handfuls of water over my head (without undoing my braids)."[5]

---

[1] Collected by Abu Daawood *(Sunan Abu Dawud* (English Trans.), vol. 1, p. 93, no. 355), an-Nasaa'ee, at-Tirmidhee and Ahmad, and rated *Saheeh* in *Irwaa al-Ghaleel*, vol. 1, pp. 163-4, no. 128.

[2] **Note for Adults:** Purification by *Ghusl* is also required in the case of wet dreams, sexual intercourse, post natal bleeding and vaginal discharge. These forms of defilement are collectively known as *al-Hadath al-Akbar*. And washing the privates and *Wudoo* is required in the case of prostatic fluid discharges.

[3] Collected by al-Bukhaaree *(Sahih Al-Bukhari* (Arabic-English), vol. 1, p. 157, no. 248), Muslim *(Sahih Muslim* (English Trans.), vol. 1, pp. 182-3, no. 616) and Abu Daawood *(Sunan Abu Dawud* (English Trans.), vol. 1, p. 61, no. 242).

[4] Reported by Maymoonah and collected by Muslim *(Sahih Muslim* (English Trans.), vol. 1, p. 61, no. 245).

[5] Collected by Muslim *(Sahih Muslim* (English Trans.), vol. 1, p. 187, no. 646).

When bathing using soap, one may complete the soaping and washing of the whole body including the hair, then proceed to make *Wuḍoo* and the complete wash. The wash may be under a shower. However, the wash should not be in a tub of standing water, because one will be washing with unclean water.

TAYAMMUM

When water is not available or in times of sickness, there is a form of purification made with clean dust, earth or sand, which takes the place of both *Wuḍoo* and *Ghusl*. It is called *Tayammum* and is done as follows:

'Ammaar reported that the Prophet (ﷺ) told him to strike both his palms on the ground once, blow on them, then wipe his face and hands, left on right, up to the wrists.[1]

---

[1] Collected by al-Bukhaaree *(Sahih Al-Bukhari* (Arabic-English), vol. 1, pp. 201-2, no. 334) and Muslim *(Sahih Muslim* (English Trans.), vol. 1, p. 202, no. 716).

QUESTIONS

1. Islamically *Tahaarah* means
   (a) hygiene or cleanliness
   (b) cleaning oneself before *Salaah* or Zakaah.
   (c) a form of cleanliness which must be made before doing certain acts of worship.
   (d) to clean one's private parts after relieving oneself and nothing else.
   (e) the acts which break one's state of purity.

2. The significance of *Tahaarah* to *Salaah* is that
   (a) *Tahaarah* increases the reward for *Salaah*.
   (b) *Tahaarah* is not accepted without *Salaah*.
   (c) *Salaah* is not accepted unless *Tahaarah* is done immediately after it.
   (d) *Tahaarah* is only done when *Salaah* is to be performed.
   (e) *Tahaarah* has to be done for *Salaah* to be accepted.

3. The main purpose behind *Tahaarah* is
   (a) to make us physically clean.
   (b) to make us spiritually clean.
   (c) to make *Wudoo*.
   (d) to teach us the importance of water.
   (e) to stop us from making *al-Hadath al-Asghar*

4. What is *al-Hadath, al-Asghar,* what causes it?

5. (a) Briefly describe the correct method for performing each of the following in point form:
      Wudoo, Ghusl and *Tayammum.*

   (b) Mention three significant differences among *Wudoo, Ghusl* and *Tayammum* in chart form.

6. It is not a part of *Wudoo* to
   (a) wipe the ears.
   (b) wipe the neck.

(c) wash between the toes.

(d) wash the fingers.

(e) wash the forehead.

7. What is the significance of *Neeyah* before making *Wuḍoo, Ghusl* or *Tayammum*.

8. *Siwaak* is recommended before every *Salaah*

   (a) because *Salaah* is not acceptable without it.

   (b) because we need to remove any particles of food from between our teeth.

   (c) to keep our teeth from getting cavities.

   (d) to keep our breath fresh so that we do not offend those praying beside us.

   (e) because it is a part of *Wuḍoo.*

16 FIQH: TOILET MANNERS

Significance.

As we learned in *Tawheed,* the whole of a Muslim's life can become *'Ebaadah* (worship), if he lives it according to the *Sunnah* of the last Prophet ( ). That is, he must make his outer actions submit to the way of life prescribed by the Prophet ( ), and he must inwardly remember Allaah in whatever he is doing. Any action which is done according to these two principles becomes a form of worship of Allaah. Therefore, according to Islaam, even the act of using the toilet can become an act of worshipping God. Since we all perform this act many times daily we should try and make it a source of blessing for us by doing it according to the *Sunnah.*

1. Du'aa before

The Prophet ( ) used to remember Allaah and seek refuge in Him by making a short prayer before going to the toilet area. The Prophet's companion, Anas ibn Maalik, reported that he used to say:

$$اللّٰهُمَّ إِنِّى أَعُوذُ بِكَ مِنَ الْخُبُثِ وَالْخَبَائِثِ$$

Allaahumma innee a'oodhu bika minal-khubuthi wal-khabaa'ith

"Oh Allaah, verily I seek refuge in You from all filth and nasty devils."[1]

This *Du'aa* serves to remind us of Allaah and to remind ourselves to avoid any filthy or indecent acts while in the bathroom or while using

---

[1] Collected in all the six books of *Hadeeth.* (*Sahih Al-Bukhari* (Arabic-English), vol. 1, pp. 105-6, no. 144), (*Sahih Muslim* (English Trans.), vol. 1, p. 205, no. 729) and (*Sunan Abu Dawud* (English Trans.), vol. 1, pp. 1-2, no. 4).

Note: Some books add بِسْمِ اللّٰه *Bismillaah* to the beginning of this *Du'aa* which only occurs in a narration collected by Ibn Abee Shaybah in *al-Musannaf.* This narration has Abu Ma'shar in its *Sanad* who is *Da'eef* (See al-Albaanee's *Tamaam al-Mannah,* pp. 56-58).

the toilet. It also provides protection from the evil *Jinn* which may harm us during times of weakness.

2. Concealment

We should not be exposed to people when we use the toilet. A companion of the Prophet (ﷺ), Jaabir reported that whenever they went out with the Prophet (ﷺ) on a trip, he would not defecate until he had concealed himself so that he could not be seen at all.[1] Ibn 'Umar also said, *"Whenever the Prophet (ﷺ) wanted to relieve himself, he would not raise his garment until he lowered himself near the ground."* [2] This was due to the fact that there were no toilets in those days, so wherever one went to relieve oneself, the possibility of being seen was always there. These principles can still be applied if similar circumstances arise during outings, etc. Where there are separate toilets or toilets within bathrooms, we should make sure that the door is properly closed when we are on the toilet, and we should not allow others to come in there with us while we use it. Based on this principle Muslim men should not use public urinals where men stand side-by-side exposing themselves and urinating. The toilets with doors should be used instead.

3. Facing the Qiblah

The companion, Abu Ayyoub al-Ansaaree, reported that the Prophet (ﷺ) said, *"If you go to defecate, do not face the **Qiblah** nor turn your back toward it. Instead, you should turn your left side or your*

---

[1] Collected by Muslim *(Sahih Muslim* (English Trans.), vol. 1, p. 162, no. 519) and Abu Daawood *(Sunan Abu Dawud* (English Trans.), vol. 1, p. 1, no. 2).

[2] There is a *Hadeeth* in which it was reported that whenever the Prophet (ﷺ) went to the toilet area he would remove his ring which had engraved on it *Muhammad, Messenger of Allaah* (Collected by Abu Daawood [*Sunan Abu Dawud*, (English Trans.), vol. 1, p. 5, no. 19], at-Tirmidhee, an-Nasaa'ee and Ibn Maajah). However, it has been rated inaccurate *(Da'eef)* by al-Albaanee in *Da'eef Sunan Ibn Maajah*, p. 24, no. 61.

right."[1] This is, however, when we are out in open areas. If we are inside the toilet, or between buildings, or behind something which shields us from the *Ka'bah*, it is allowable to face the *Qiblah* or put our backs to it when relieving ourselves. Ibn 'Umar said, *"One day when I climbed on top of Hafsah's house, I saw the Prophet (ﷺ) relieving himself facing Shaam[2] with his back towards **Ka'bah.**"*[3] Marwaan al-Asfar reported that when he saw Ibn 'Umar make his camel kneel and then he urinated towards the *Qiblah*, he said, "Oh 'Abdur-Rahmaan, has that not been forbidden in open places?" He replied, "If there is between you and the *Qiblah* something shielding you, there is no harm in it."[4] Because we pray to Allaah facing the *Qiblah*, where the first house of worship is situated, we do not relieve ourselves in the same direction or while turning our backs to it out of the honor and respect that we hold for it.

4. Squatting

It is *Mustahaab* (recommended) that we use the toilet in the sitting position and not standing, particularly when urinating. It was the practice of the Arabs in the time of the Prophet (ﷺ) to urinate standing. Consequently, they used to make fun of the Prophet (ﷺ) if they came across him urinating squatting. 'Abdur-Rahmaan ibn Hasanah said, " 'Amr and I went to see the Prophet (ﷺ). He came out with a leather shield in his hand, screened himself with it and uri-

---

[1] Collected by al-Bukhaaree *(Sahih Al-Bukhari* (Arabic-English), vol. 1, p. 106, no. 146), Muslim *(Sahih Muslim* (English Trans.), vol. 1, p. 160, no. 507) and Abu Daawood *(Sunan Abu Dawud* (English Trans.), vol. 1, p. 3, no. 9).

[2] Syria i.e., Northerly.

[3] Collected by al-Bukhaaree *(Sahih Al-Bukhari* (Arabic-English), vol. 1, p. 108, no. 150, Muslim *(Sahih Muslim* (English Trans.), vol. 1, p. 161, no. 510) and Abu Daawood *(Sunan Abu Dawud* (English Trans.), vol. 1, p. 3, no. 12).

[4] Collected by Abu Daawood *(Sunan Abu Dawud* (English Trans.), vol. 1, p. 3, no. 11), an-Nasaa'ee and Ibn Maajah and rated Saheeh authentic *(Hasan)* in *Saheeh Sunan Abee Daawood*, vol. 1, p. 5, no. 8.

nated. We said, 'Look at him urinating like a woman!' "[1] This was the general practice of the Prophet (ﷺ) and because of that 'Aa'eshah said, "Do not believe anyone who tells you that Allaah's messenger urinated standing. He only urinated sitting."[2] This was the only way that she had observed him, but there were other rare occasions on which the Prophet (ﷺ) did do so. The Prophet's companion Hudhayfah reported that on one occasion the Prophet (ﷺ) went near the garbage dump of a tribe and urinated standing.[3] Thus, it is not *Haraam* to do so, but it is preferable to urinate in the sitting position. The medical profession has confirmed that the squatting position is the healthiest position for relieving oneself.

5. Splatter

Great care should be taken to avoid the splatter of urine on one's clothing or body, because one would remain unclean even if *Wudoo* were performed afterwards. Ibn 'Abbaas said, *"Allaah's Messenger (ﷺ) passed by two graves and said, 'Both are being punished! They are not being punished for major (sins). One did not shield himself from urine and the other carried gossip."* [4] The recommendation for urinating squatting helps us to avoid excessive splatter of urine. Based on this principle urinals should be avoided wherever possible and where necessary they should be flushed during use to avoid the splatter of urine.

---

[1] Collected by Abu Dawood *(Sunan Abu Dawud* (English Trans.), vol. 1, p. 6, no. 22), an-Nasaa'ee and Ibn Maajah and rated *Saheeh* in *Saheeh Sunan Abee Daawood*, vol. 1, p. 7, no. 16.

[2] Collected by at-Tirmidhee, an-Nasaa'ee and Ibn Maajah and rated *Saheeh* in *Saheeh Sunan at-Tirmidhee*, vol. 1, p. 6, no. 11.

[3] Collected by at-Tirmidhee, Ibn Maajah and Abu Daawood *(Sunan Abu Dawud* (English Trans.), vol. 1, p. 6, no. 23) and rated *Saheeh* in *Saheeh Sunan at-Tirmidhee*, vol. 1, p. 6, no. 12.

[4] Collected by al-Bukhaaree *(Sahih Al-Bukhari* (Arabic-English), vol. 1, p. 142, no. 217), Muslim *(Sahih Muslim* (English Trans.), vol. 1, p. 171-2, no. 575) and Abu Daawood *(Sunan Abu Dawud* (English Trans.), vol. 1, p. 5, no. 20).

6. Conversation

It is preferable to avoid any form of conversation when on the toilet as Ibn 'Umar reported that a man passed by Allaah's messenger while he was urinating and greeted him with *Salaams*, but the Prophet (ﷺ) did not return them.[1] Since the Prophet (ﷺ) refused to return *Salaams* which is among the rights of a Muslim on his brother, it shows that it is better not to return *Salaams* or to engage in conversation.[2] However, this only applies to the case where one is actually on the toilet, otherwise it is allowable to answer or converse with others while one is in the bathroom. As for the *Salaams*, they may be returned after purification, as al-Muhaajir ibn Qunfudh said, *"I gave* **Salaams** *to the Prophet (ﷺ) while he was urinating and he did not return them until he made* **Wuḍoo**. *When he (completed) the* **Wuḍoo** *he returned them."*[3]

7. Prohibited Places

One should not relieve oneself in places commonly used by the public. Abu Hurayrah reported that Allaah's Messenger (ﷺ) said, *"Be on your guard against two acts which provoke cursing."* Those present asked, *'What are they O Messenger of Allaah (ﷺ)?'* He replied, *"Relieving oneself in roads where people walk and in the shade (where they take shelter and rest)."*[1]

---

[1] Collected by Muslim and Abu Daawood *(Sunan Abu Dawud* (English Trans.), vol. 1, p. 4, no. 16) and rated *Ṣaḥeeh* in *Ṣaḥeeh Sunan Abee Daawood*, vol. 1, p. 6, no. 12.

[2] There is a *Hadeeth* reported by Abu Sa'eed in which he was supposed to have said, "I heard Allaah's Messenger (ﷺ) say, *'Allaah is angry when two people go and defecate together exposing their privates and talking with each other.'* " (Collected by Abu Daawood *(Sunan Abu Dawud* (English Trans.), vol. 1, p. 4, no. 15), however it is very weak *(Da'eef)* and can not be used as evidence. See *Tamaam al-Mannah*, pp. 58-9.

[3] Collected by an-Nasaa'ee and rated *Ṣaḥeeh* by al-Albaanee in *Ṣaḥeeh Sunan an-Nasaa'ee*, vol. 1, p. 10, no. 37.

[4] Collected by Muslim *(Sahih Muslim* (English Trans.), vol. 1, p. 162, no. 516) and Abu Daawood *(Sunan Abu Dawud* (English Trans.), vol. 1, p. 7, no. 25).

It is also prohibited to relieve oneself in standing water as others may use it. Jaabir reported that Allaah's Messenger (ﷺ) forbade that one should urinate in standing water.[1] Consequently, one should not pass urine while in swimming pools.

The Prophet (ﷺ) also forbade us from urinating in water and bathing in it. Abu Hurayrah reported that Allaah's Messenger (ﷺ) said, *"None of you should urinate in standing water, and then bathe (make **Ghusl**) in it."*[2]

8. Cleaning method

(a) The Hand

The left hand is reserved for touching the private parts when cleaning away feces and urine. The Prophet (ﷺ) forbade the use of the right which has been reserved for eating and drinking. Abu Qataadah reported that Allaah's messenger (ﷺ) said, *"None of you should touch his privates with his right hand while urinating nor should he wipe off feces with his right."*[3] If the same hand were used for both eating and cleaning it may be quite unhealthy.

(b) Material

After relieving oneself, the remaining feces or urine should be removed with either dry material, like toilet paper, or with water. It is however preferable to use both water and dry material as it was the regular practice of the Prophet (ﷺ) to do so. Anas ibn Maalik reported that whenever Allaah's messenger (ﷺ) went to the toilet

---

[1] Collected by Muslim *(Sahih Muslim* (English Trans.), vol. 1, p. 167, no. 553).

[2] Collected by Muslim *(Sahih Muslim* (English Trans.), vol. 1, p. 167, no. 554), and Abu Daawood *(Sunan Abu Dawud* (English Trans.), vol. 1, pp. 17-8, no. 69) and by Abu Daawood *(Sunan Abu Dawud* (English Trans.), vol. 1, p. 7, no. 27) from 'Abdullaah ibn al-Mughaffal.

[3] Collected in all the six books of *Hadeeth.* *(Sahih Al-Bukhari* (Arabic-English), vol. 1, p. 110, no. 155, *(Sahih Muslim* (English Trans.), vol. 1, p. 161, no. 513 and *(Sunan Abu Dawud* (English Trans.), vol. 1, p. 8, no. 31).

area he would carry a small leather water pouch and the Prophet
(ﷺ) would clean himself with the water.[1]

(c) Number of Times

If dry material is used to remove the waste matter, the area should be
wiped at least three times with clean pieces of material in order to
ensure that it is properly cleaned. Since toilet paper was not available
in the Prophet's (ﷺ) day he insisted that no less than three pebbles
be used. Salmaan al-Faarisee reported that the Prophet (ﷺ) forbade them from facing the *Qiblah* when urinating or defecating,
cleaning themselves with their right hands and using less than three
pebbles.[2]

9. Du'aa After

When the Prophet (ﷺ) left the toilet area, he used to ask Allaah's
pardon. 'Aa'eshah reported that he used to say, غُفْرَانَك *"Ghuf-
raanak* (I beg Your forgiveness)." [3]

---

[1] Collected by al-Bukhaaree *(Sahih Al-Bukhari* (Arabic-English), vol. 1, p. 109,
no. 152), Muslim and Abu Daawood *(Sunan Abu Dawud* (English Trans.), vol. 1,
p. 10, no. 43).

[2] Collected by Muslim, *(Sahih Muslim* (English Trans.), vol. 1, p. 160, no. 504),
Abu Daawood *(Sunan Abu Dawud* (English Trans.), vol. 1, p. 2, no. 7) and at-Tirmidhee.

[3] Collected by Abu Daawood, *(Sunan Abu Dawud* (English Trans.), vol. 1, pp. 7-8,
no. 30) at-Tirmidhee, Ibn Maajah, ad-Daarimee and Ahmad and rated *Saheeh* in
Saheeh at-Tirmidhee, vol. 1, p. 5, no. 7.

Note: The *Du'aa* collected by, Ibn Maajah and narrated by Anas ibn Maalik
wherein the Prophet (ﷺ) was supposed to have said, *"Al-Hamdu lillaah
alladhee adh-haba 'annil-adhaa wa 'aafaanee* (All praise is due to Allaah who
removed from me the harm and restored my health)" is not authentic (See
Tamaam al-Munnah, p. 66, no. 15). Likewise, Ibn Umar's narration *"Al-Hamdu
lillaah alladhee adhaaqanee ladhdhatah wa abqaa feeya quwaatah wa adh-haba
'annee adhaah* (Praise be to Allaah who let me enjoy it, kept for me its energy and
relieved me of its harm)" Collected by Ibn as-Sunnee and at-Tabaraanee.

10. Stepping in and out

It was also the practice of the Prophet (ﷺ) to step into the toilet area with his left foot and out of it with his right. This was because the right side of the body is given preference over the left in all acts which are considered pleasing and nice while the left is used for those which are considered nasty. 'Aa'eshah reported that the Prophet (ﷺ) used to like to begin with his right side in wearing shoes, combing his hair, *Tahaarah* (purification) and in all his affairs.[1] This may be related to the Divine fact that whoever gets his book of deeds in his right hand will go to Paradise, while he who receives it in his left will go to Hell. Allaah said:

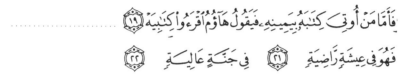

"Then he who will be given his record (of deeds) in his right hand will say, 'Ah here! Read all of you my record....and he will be in a pleasant life in a lofty garden."

(Soorah al-Ḥaaqqah (69):19 & 21-22)

فَأَمَّا مَنْ أُوتِيَ كِتَابَهُ بِشِمَالِهِ فَيَقُولُ يَلَيْتَنِي لَمْ أُوتَ كِتَابِيَهُ ﴿٢٥﴾ خُذُوهُ فَغُلُّوهُ ﴿٣٠﴾ ثُمَّ الْجَحِيمَ صَلُّوهُ ﴿٣١﴾

"And he who is given his record (of deeds) in his left hand will say, 'Ah! If only my record were not given to me'...(It will be said) 'Sieze him and bind him, and burn him in a blazing fire.' "

(Soorah al-Ḥaaqqah (69):25 & 30-31)

---

[1] Collected by al-Bukhaaree (*Sahih Al-Bukhari* (Arabic-English), vol. 1, p. 117-8, no. 169).

Thus, the practice of preference of the right serves to remind us of Allaah and the Judgement. It also gives our lives a system. Things done according to a system are always superior to things which are haphazardly done. This system helps to train us in obedience to the way of the Prophet (ﷺ) which is the key to success in both this life and the next, and it encourages us to choose the right over the wrong in this life.

QUESTIONS

1. What are the two basic conditions for turning any act into an act of worship?

2. The *Du'aa* for entering the toilet is
   (a) Ghafraanak! al-Hamdu lil-laah minal-khubuthi wal-khabaa-ith
   (b) al-Hamdu lil-laah a'oodhu bika minal-khubuthi wal-khabaa-ith.
   (c) A'oodhu bika minal-Khabaa-ith wa 'aafanee.
   (d) Allaahummaa innee a'oodhu bika minal-Khabaa-ith wa 'aafanee.
   (e) Allaahumma innee a'oodhu bika minal-Khubuthi wal-Khabaa-ith.

3. This Du'aa means
   (a) Oh Allaah, verily I seek refuge in You from filth and bad health.
   (b) All praise is due to Allaah who saved me from filth and nasty deeds.
   (c) Oh Allaah, verily I ask Your pardon from filth and nasty deeds.
   (d) All praise is Allaah's who gave me refuge from nasty deeds and restored my health.
   (e) Oh Allaah, verily I seek refuge in You from filth and nasty devils.

4. We should step into the bathroom with our (left/right) foot first and leave the bathroom with our (left/right) foot last.

5. What should we do before removing our clothes to use the toilet?
   (a) Turn off the bathroom light.
   (b) Make sure that the bathroom door is wide open.
   (c) Turn our backs toward the *Qiblah*.
   (d) Close the bathroom door properly.
   (e) Take off our shoes.

6. When we are relieving ourselves outside in open areas we should
   (a) face the *Qiblah*.
   (b) turn our backs to the *Qiblah*.
   (c) turn our right or left side to the *Qiblah*.
   (d) not turn our right or left side to the *Qiblah*.
   (e) step into the area with our right foot.

7. (a) While using the toilet, one should (talk/not talk) to others.

   (b) What are the three main places in which it is forbidden to relieve oneself?

8. The Islamic position on squatting while relieving oneself is that
   (a) it is recommended when defecating but not when urinating.
   (b) one should do so when facing the *Qiblah* but otherwise it is not necessary.
   (c) the Prophet (鑾) recommended it for the old and sickly.
   (d) it is disliked for males and recommended for females.
   (e) it is preferable to do so.

9. When cleaning oneself after using the toilet, one should
   (a) use the left hand for pouring water and the right for cleaning.
   (b) use paper and water but not paper alone.
   (c) use water, paper or both.
   (d) use the right hand for removing feces and the left for washing away urine.
   (e) not use water alone.

10. Briefly explain two reasons why we only use one hand to clean ourselves.

10. What is the *Du'aa* said when leaving the toilet?

11. The main purpose of saying *Du'aas* before entering the toilet and after leaving it is to
   (a) take our minds of what we are doing.
   (b) remind us of which foot to use in entering and leaving.
   (c) remind us of Allaah.

(d) prepare us for an act of worship.

(e) make us enter and exit slowly.

12. Two reasons for stepping in and out of the bathroom according to the method used by the Prophet (ﷺ) are that

(a) it reminds to make *wuḍoo* and it makes wearing our shoes easier.

(b) it gives our life value and direction.

(c) it reminds us of Allaah and causes us to forget satan.

(d) it protects us from satan and nasty deeds.

(e) it gives our life a system and it reminds us of the Day of Judgement.

17. FIQH: ZAKAAH

Meaning

Literally the term "*Zakaah*" means growth or purity, however, in Islaam, *Zakaah* refers to a form of charity which has to be paid on certain amounts of wealth. This form of charity was called *Zakaah* because the blessings on the remaining wealth are increased by Allaah even though the actual quantity of wealth has decreased. Allaah says in the Qur'aan:

$$يَمۡحَقُ ٱللَّهُ ٱلرِّبَوٰاْ وَيُرۡبِي ٱلصَّدَقَٰتِۗ وَٱللَّهُ لَا يُحِبُّ كُلَّ كَفَّارٍ أَثِيمٍ$$

"Allaah will deprive interest *(Ribaa)* of its blessing, but He will cause the blessings of charity *(Sadaqah)* to increase"
(Soorah al-Baqarah (2):276)

The Prophet Muhammad (ﷺ) said, "*Anyone of you who gives charity from honestly-earned wealth–and Allaah only accepts good–Allaah, The Most Merciful, will take it in His right hand. And if it is only a date, it will grow in the palm of the Most Merciful until it becomes bigger than a mountain, in the same way as one of you rears his young colt or his young camel.*"[1] This form of charity also purifies the one who gives it of greed.

Classification

Zakaah is considered to be *Waajib* (a compulsory duty) on all Muslims who fulfill the conditions necessary for its payment. The proof that it is *Waajib* can be found in both the Qur'aan and the *Sunnah*. In the Qur'aan, Allaah said,

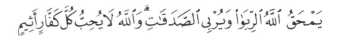

$$وَءَاتُواْ ٱلزَّكَوٰةَ$$

---

[1] Narrated by Abu Hurayrah and collected by al-Bukhaaree (*Sahih Al-Bukhari* (Arabic-English), vol. 2, p. 281, no. 491), Muslim *(Sahih Muslim* (English Trans.), vol. 2, p. 485-6, no. 2211) and at-Tirmidhee. The wording is at-Tirmidhee's.

"...and all of you (should) give *Zakaah.*"

(Soorah al-Baqarah (2):43)

In the *Sunnah*, the Prophet (ﷺ) told Mu'aadh ibn Jabal, *"Teach them (the people of Yemen) that Allaah has made **Sadaqah** (charity) compulsory on them. It should be taken from the rich among them and given to their poor."*[1]

Significance

The principle of *Zakaah* is of great importance to the system of Islaam and the following points are only a few of the many which could be mentioned to show the great importance of *Zakaah.*

1. *Zakaah* is considered the third most important pillar of Islaam. The Prophet (ﷺ) listed the five pillars of Islaam as follows: *"Is-laam is built on five: Declaring that there is no god but Allaah and that Muhammad is His servant and messenger; establishing **Salaah;** paying **Zakaah;** fasting the month of Ramadaan and going on **Hajj** to the House (**Ka'bah**) if one is able."*[2] It should also be noted that whenever Allaah mentions the order to establish *Salaah*, He usually adds the order to pay *Zakaah.* For example,

$$ وَمَآ أُمِرُوٓا۟ إِلَّا لِيَعْبُدُوا۟ ٱللَّهَ مُخْلِصِينَ لَهُ ٱلدِّينَ حُنَفَآءَ وَيُقِيمُوا۟ ٱلصَّلَوٰةَ وَيُؤْتُوا۟ ٱلزَّكَوٰةَ ۚ وَذَٰلِكَ دِينُ ٱلْقَيِّمَةِ $$

"And they (former nations) were ordered to sincerely worship Allaah alone, to establish *Salaah*, pay *Zakaah* and that is the correct form of religion."

(Soorah al-Bayyinah (98):5)

---

[1] Reported by Ibn 'Abbaas and collected by al-Bukhaaree (*Sahih Al-Bukhari* (Arabic-English), vol. 2, pp. 271-2, no. 478) and Muslim *(Sahih Muslim* (English Trans.), vol. 1, pp. 14, no. 27).

[2] Collected by al-Bukhaaree (*Sahih Al-Bukhari* (Arabic-English), vol. 1, pp. 9-10, no. 18) and Muslim *(Sahih Muslim* (English Trans.), vol. 1, p. 17, no. 7).

2. *Zakaah* is so important in Islaam that any Muslim who claims that *Zakaah* is not a compulsory duty in Islaam can be executed by the state if he does not repent and take back what he said. This ruling is based on the unanimous agreement *(Ijmaa')* of the Ṣaḥaabah to fight those Muslims who refused to pay *Zakaah* after the death of the Prophet Muḥammad (ﷺ).[1]

3. State care for the weak and poor is based on the collection of *Zakaah*. The funds of the *Bayt al-Maal* (central treasury of the Islamic state) come mostly from the collection of *Zakaah*. And it is from these funds that the Islamic state looks after the needs of the poorer members of society. In former times, the state was controlled by the rich and taxes collected from the poor and working classes went into the pockets of the rulers. However, in the Islamic system it is just the opposite. Money is collected from the rich and given to the weak and poor members of society.

4. *Zakaah* also keeps wealth circulating in society resulting in the growth of businesses and an increase in the number of jobs available. If wealth is taken out of circulation by hoarding, more *Zakaah* has to be paid on it than if it were invested. Therefore, the wealthy are forced to keep their wealth working for themselves, as well as for the society, in order to protect it from being eaten all up by *Zakaah*.

Purpose

Zakaah is a form of worship which has as its main goal the spiritual development of the Believer just as in the case of *Salaah*, *Ṣawm* etc. Therefore, it should not be looked at as being only an economic duty. The spiritual purpose for *Zakaah* is recorded in the following Qur'anic verse:

$$\text{خُذْ مِنْ أَمْوَالِهِمْ صَدَقَةً تُطَهِّرُهُمْ وَتُزَكِّيهِم بِهَا وَصَلِّ عَلَيْهِمْ}$$

---

[1] See *Sahih Al-Bukhari* (Arabic-English), vol. 2, p. 274, no. 483 and *Sunan Abu Dawud* (English Trans.), vol. 2, p. 403, no. 1551.

"Take _Sadaqah_ from their wealth in order to purify them and make them grow..."

(Soorah at-Tawbah (9):103)

The wealth which the rich give helps to cleanse their hearts of greed, stinginess and the excessive love of the pleasures of this world. It also trains them to be generous with the wealth which Allaah has blessed them with, thereby contributing to their spiritual growth. At the same time, the wealth which is given to the poor and unfortunate members of society helps to mend their hearts by removing some of the natural jealousy and hatred which they hold for the rich.

Conditions

For _Zakaah_ to be _Waajib,_ the following four conditions have to be met.

1. One should be a sane Muslim above the age of puberty. There is no obligation on non-Muslims to pay _Zakaah_ even though they may be among those who receive it. Because _Zakaah_ is a form of worship, it must have along with it the correct belief in Allaah for it to be accepted. What is obligatory on the non-Muslim is the acceptance of Islaam. As for the insane and the child, there is no obligation since they are not considered responsible for their actions due to their mental state. The Prophet (ﷺ) laid down this principle in the statement which follows: _"The pen (which records deeds) is raised from the book (of deeds) for three people: The child until he becomes a youth, the sleeper until he awakes and the insane until he regains his sanity."_[1]

2. One should have in his possession money or wealth over and above his basic needs. If one has money left over after looking after his basic needs such as food, clothing, housing, transportation, etc., as

---

[1] Narrated by 'Aa'eshah and collected by Abu Daawood, _(Sunan Abu Dawud_ (English Trans.), vol. 3, p. 1226, no. 4384), at-Tirmidhee and Ibn Maajah, and rated _Saheeh_ in _Saheeh Sunan at-Tirmidhee,_ vol. 2, p. 64, no. 1150.

well as the needs of his family, that surplus wealth then becomes eligible for the extraction of *Zakaah.*

3. One should have surplus wealth above the minimum exemption limit *(Nisaab),* the lowest amount of wealth on which the payment of *Zakaah* is due. Abu Sa'eed reported that Allaah's Messenger (ﷺ) said, *"No **Zakaah** is due on property valued at less than five Ooqeeyahs of silver (400 gms.), or less than five camels, and on less than five **Wasqs** (1000 kgms.) of food grains."*[1] Anyone who does not possess surplus wealth above the *Nisaab* is considered poor and thus eligible to receive *Zakaah.*

4. One has to possess excess wealth above the *Nisaab* for the period of a year before he is required to pay *Zakaah.* Ibn 'Umar reported that Allaah's Messenger (ﷺ) said, *"Whoever acquires wealth is not obliged to pay **Zakaah** until a year has passed on it."*[2] In the case of agricultural produce, *Zakaah* known as *'Ushr* is paid at the time of harvesting if it is above the *Nisaab,* regardless of whether a year has passed on it or not. Allaah said in the Qur'aan:

وَهُوَ ٱلَّذِىٓ أَنشَأَ جَنَّٰتٍ مَّعۡرُوشَٰتٍ وَغَيۡرَ مَعۡرُوشَٰتٍ وَٱلنَّخۡلَ وَٱلزَّرۡعَ مُخۡتَلِفًا أُكُلُهُۥ وَٱلزَّيۡتُونَ وَٱلرُّمَّانَ مُتَشَٰبِهًا وَغَيۡرَ مُتَشَٰبِهٍ كُلُوا۟ مِن ثَمَرِهِۦٓ إِذَآ أَثۡمَرَ وَءَاتُوا۟ حَقَّهُۥ يَوۡمَ حَصَادِهِۦ وَلَا تُسۡرِفُوٓا۟

"It is He Who produces gardens trellised and untrellised, the dates and crops of various flavors, olives and pomegranates, like and unlike. Eat of their fruit in their season, but pay its due on the harvest day."

(Soorah al-An'aam (6):141)

---

[1] Collected by al-Bukhaaree *(Sahih Al-Bukhari* (Arabic-English), vol. 2, p. 277, no. 487).

[2] Collected by at-Tirmidhee and Ibn Maajah and rated *Saheeh* in *Saheeh Sunan at-Tirmidhee,* vol. 1, p. 196, no. 515.

Niṣaab and Rate

The *Nisaab* for various forms of wealth varies and so does the rate of *Zakaah*. The rate of *Zakaah* is the actual amount which must be paid if the *Nisaab* is reached. Both the *Nisaabs* and the rates were fixed by the Prophet (ﷺ) himself and the following table is a simplified chart for calculating the *Zakaah* on most forms of wealth.

WEALTH	NIṢAAB	RATE
Gold	2 ounces	2.5%
Silver	14 1/2 ounces	2.5%
Currency	Same as the value of the *Nisaab* for gold i.e. approx $1,000	2.5%
Trade Goods	Same as gold	2.5%
Jewellery[1]	Same as gold	2.5%
Sheep or Goats	40	1 sheep or goat
Cows	30	1 year-old calf
Camels	5	1 sheep or goat
Farm Produce	2,000 lbs	10% if the land is naturally irrigated and 5% if it is artificially irrigated

---

[1] There is a difference of opinion among scholars which goes back to the time of the *Sahaabah* about whether women have to pay *Zakaah* on gold and silver jewellery which they wear. However, evidence from *Hadeeth* support those who hold that *Zakaah* must be paid. The following are only two of many examples.

'Amr ibn Shu'ayb reported the following from his father from his grandfather: "*A woman accompanied by her daughter came to Allaah's Messenger (ﷺ) wearing*

For example, if the conditions for the payment of *Zakaah* are met and an individual has surplus wealth of 200 ounces of gold in his possession, he would have to pay 200 x 2.5/100 = 5 ounces of gold, or 5 x $500 (the value of 1 oz of gold) = $2,500.

Distribution

Allaah in the Qur'aan clearly identified those who should receive *Zakaah*. He said,

$$إِنَّمَا ٱلصَّدَقَٰتُ لِلْفُقَرَآءِ وَٱلْمَسَٰكِينِ وَٱلْعَٰمِلِينَ عَلَيْهَا وَٱلْمُؤَلَّفَةِ قُلُوبُهُمْ وَفِى ٱلرِّقَابِ وَٱلْغَٰرِمِينَ وَفِى سَبِيلِ ٱللَّهِ وَٱبْنِ ٱلسَّبِيلِ فَرِيضَةً مِّنَ ٱللَّهِ وَٱللَّهُ عَلِيمٌ حَكِيمٌ$$

"As a matter of fact, the distribution of *Zakaah* is only for the needy, the indigent, the *Zakaah* officials, for those whose hearts are to be won over, for ransoming slaves, helping the debtors, for those in Allaah's path and for the traveller.

---

two heavy gold bangles on her arms. He asked her, 'Do you pay **Zakaah** *on them? She replied, 'No.' He then said, 'Would you like Allaah to put two bangles of fire on your arms?' "* Collected by Abu Daawood *(Sunan Abu Dawud* (English Trans.), vol. 2, p. 405-6, no. 1558), an-Nasaa'ee, at-Tirmidhee and Aḥmad, and rated *Ṣaheeh* in *Ṣaheeh Sunan at-Tirmidhee*, vol. 1, p. 198, no. 518).

Umm Salamah also said, *"I used to wear gold jewellery so I asked, 'Is this considered* **Kanz** *(wealth on which Zakaah is due) Oh Messenger of Allaah (ﷺ)?' He replied, 'Whatever of it reaches the* **Zakaah** *requirement, is not* **Kanz** *if you pay it.' "* Collected by Abu Daawood *(Sunan Abu Dawud* (English Trans.), vol. 2, p. 406, no. 1559) and rated authentic *(Ḥasan)* in *Ṣaheeh Sunan Abee Daawood*, vol. 1, p. 291, no. 1383).

The *Hadeeth* most often quoted by those who excuse women from paying *Zakaah* on jewellery is that of Jaabir in which Prophet (ﷺ) was supposed to have said, *"There is no* **Zakaah** *due on jewellery."* It was collected by Ibn al-Jawzee in *at-Tahqeeq* and it is false. The authentic narrations show it to be a statement of Jaabir and not the Prophet (ﷺ). See *Irwaa al-Ghaleel*, vol. 3, p. 294-5, no. 817.

This is an obligatory duty assigned by Allaah, and Allaah is all knowing, all wise."

(Soorah at-Tawbah (9):60)

Thus, the distribution of *Zakaah* is not left solely to the state. The duty of the state is to collect *Zakaah,* find those who are in most need from among the categories identified by Allaah, and distribute the *Zakaah* among them. The following is a brief explanation of each of the categories of those eligible for receiving *Zakaah.*

1. The Needy (al-Fuqaraa)

A person is considered *Faqeer* (needy) if he has to depend on others for his daily bread. This includes all helpless people who need financial help and co-operation from others, whether temporarily or permanently. Thus, *Zakaah* can be spent to help invalids, orphans, widows, old people, the jobless and those who have been afflicted by unforseen calamity. They may all be given temporary or permanent allowances according to their needs, and homes may also be built and people hired to look after them.

2. The Indigent (al-Masaakeen)

The Prophet (ﷺ) explained what was meant by this category as follows: *"He who does not get enough to satisfy his needs, but is neither recognized to be poor nor does he beg, is an indigent."*[1] From this *Hadeeth* we may conclude that the indigent are those who are very poor, but due to their self-respect they neither beg nor request help from others. The Islamic state or community is obliged to find these people by careful investigation in order to see that their needs are met.

3. The Zakaah Officials (al-'Aamileena alayhaa)

This refers to the official agents appointed by the Islamic govern-

---

[1] Collected by al-Bukhaaree (*Sahih Al-Bukhari* (Arabic-English), vol. 2, p. 324, no. 557) and Muslim (*Sahih Muslim* (English Trans.), vol. 2, pp. 496-7, no. 2261).

ment or community to collect and distribute *Zakaah*, as well as maintain the *Zakaah* accounts of the community or state. Their salaries are taken from the *Zakaah* funds, regardless of whether they possess the *Nisaab* or not. Abu Humayd as-Saa'idee reported that Allaah's Messenger (ﷺ) appointed a man called al-Lutbeeyah from the Asd tribe to collect *Zakaah* from the Sulaym tribe, and when he returned, he paid him.[1]

4. Winning Over Hearts (al-Mu'allafah Quloobuhum)

This term is in reference to those whose hearts may be won over to Islaam by material incentives due to the fact that they already lean towards it. For example, they may be non-Muslims or newly converted Muslims whose faith in Islaam is not yet strong enough to encourage them to serve the interest of Islaam and the Islamic community. It was the practice of the Prophet (ﷺ) to encourage those who had any interest in Islaam by offering them a share in the spoils of war in the hope that they would accept Islaam and they would later understand and practice the spiritual principles which lay behind it. After the Battle of Hunayn (630 CE) the Prophet (ﷺ) gave most of the spoils to non-Muslim Makkans who had joined forces with the Muslims. When his companions questioned him he replied, *"I gave to persons who were quite recently in a state of unbelief, so that I may incline them to the truth. Don't you feel pleased that those people go with riches and you go back to your places with the Messenger of Allaah?"*[2] Such people may also be given money out of *Zakaah* funds even if they are well-to-do.

5. Ransoming Slaves (Fee ar-Riqaab)

Zakaah may also be used to buy the freedom of Muslims who are prisoners of war, or slaves in a society which allows slavery. If,

---

[1] Collected by al-Bukhaaree (*Sahih Al-Bukhari* (Arabic-English), vol. 2, p. 337, no. 576).

[2] Reported by Anas and collected by Muslim (*Sahih Muslim* (English Trans.), vol. 2, p. 505-6, no. 2303).

however, there are no prisoners of war nor slaves, this category would be overlooked until such conditions arise.

6. Debtors (al-Ghaarimoon)

This category refers to those people who are so heavily in debt that there is no way for them to save enough money to pay off their debts. *Zakaah* funds can be used to help relieve them of their debts, whether they are working, or unemployed due to a lack of work or some physical disability.

7. In Allaah's Path (Fee Sabeelillaah)

The phrase *"in Allaah's path"* applies first and foremost to *Jihaad* (war against the forces of disbelief) and includes all efforts made by Muslims to establish the Islamic order in the place of un-Islamic systems. Thus, *Zakaah* funds can also be used to equip soldiers committed to *Jihaad*. This category has also been generalized by some scholars to include all efforts aimed at spreading the message of Islaam *(Da'wah)*, thereby including the printing of Islamic literature and so on.

Pilgrims to Makkah who have become stranded due to some unforseen accident, as well as needy students who are seeking religious knowledge, can also be included in this category. They both have the right to receive help from *Zakaah* funds according to their specific needs.

8. Travellers (Ibn as-Sabeel)

This applies to any traveller who has become stranded due to a lack of funds or the occurrence of a misfortune. Such an individual can also be given help from *Zakaah* funds in order to help him continue on his way, whether he has money at home or not. This principle may also be expanded to include the cost of setting up hostels for travellers.

QUESTIONS

1. Literally *Zakaah* means
   (a) money.
   (b) charity.
   (c) growth.
   (d) *Waajib*.
   (e) The minimum exemption limit.

2. Islamically *Zakaah* refers to
   (a) charity paid twice per year on all wealth.
   (b) money paid to the government as taxes on one's earnings.
   (c) money paid to the poor at the beginning of the Ramadaan fast.
   (d) charity which must be paid on certain amounts of wealth.
   (e) a form of voluntary charity given to the poor.

3. How does *Zakaah* increase wealth of one who pays it?

4. Briefly explain four points showing the significance of *Zakaah*.

5. List and briefly explain the four conditions for the obligation of *Zakaah*.

6. The main purpose of *Zakaah* in the case of wealthy people is to
   (a) make them poor.
   (b) remove the natural jealousy in their hearts for the poor.
   (c) cleanse them of generosity.
   (d) cleanse their hearts of greed.
   (e) distribute their wealth.

7. Mention briefly three differences between *'Ushr* and *Zakaah* on wealth.

8. The rate of *Zakaah* for money is
   (a) 2.5 %.
   (b) 5.2 %.
   (c) .25 %.
   (d) 25 %.
   (d) 2 ounces.

9. If a man had $40,000 of excess wealth for half a year how much *Zakaah* would he have to pay?

   (a) $1000.
   (b) $10,000.
   (c) $100,000.
   (d) $200.
   (e) none.

10. How much *Zakaah* would a man who had $8,000 saved for a year have to pay?

   (a) $20,000.
   (b) $2,000.
   (c) $200.
   (d) $1,000.
   (e) none.

11. *Zakaah* may be distributed
   (a) according to the needs of the Islamic state.
   (b) only to the poor and the indigent.
   (c) only to the eight categories of peqple defined in the Qur'aan.
   (d) to gamblers with large debts, too great for them to repay.
   (e) among Muslims only.

18. FIQH: ZAKAAH AL-FIṬR

Meaning

Zakaah al-Fiṭr is often referred to as *Ṣadaqah al-Fiṭr*. The word *Fiṭr* means the same as *Iftaar*, breaking a fast, and it comes from the same root as the word *Futoor* which means breakfast. Thus, Islamically, *Zakaah al-Fiṭr* is the name given to charity which is distributed at the end of the fast of Ramadaan.

Classification

Ṣadaqah al-Fiṭr is a duty which is *Waajib* on every Muslim, whether male or female, minor or adult, as long as he has the means to do so. The proof that this form of charity is compulsory can be found in the *Sunnah* whereby Ibn 'Umar reported that the Prophet (ﷺ) made *Zakaah al-Fiṭr* compulsory on every slave, freeman, male, female, young and old among Muslims; one *Saa'* of dried dates or one *Saa'* of barley.[1] The head of the household may pay the required amount for the other members. Abu Sa'eed al-Khudree said, *"On behalf of our young and old, free men and slaves, we used to take out during Allaah's Messenger's (ﷺ) lifetime one Saa' of grain, cheese or raisins."*[2]

Significance

The significant role played by *Zakaah* in the circulation of wealth within the Islamic society is also played by *Ṣadaqah al-Fiṭr*. However, in the case of *Ṣadaqah al-Fiṭr*, each individual is required to calculate how much charity is due from himself and his dependents and go into the community in order to find those who deserve such charity. Thus, *Ṣadaqah al-Fiṭr* plays a very important role in the development of the bonds of community. The rich are obliged to

---

[1] Collected by al-Bukhaaree (*Sahih Al-Bukhari* (Arabic-English), vol. 2, p. 339, no. 579), Muslim (*Sahih Muslim* (English Trans.), vol. 2, p. 468, no. 2149) and Abu Daawood (*Sunan Abu Dawud* (English Trans.), vol. 2, p. 422, no. 1607 and 1608).

[2] Collected by Muslim (*Sahih Muslim* (English Trans.), vol. 2, p. 469, no. 2155).

come in direct contact with the poor, and the poor are put in contact with the extremely poor. This contact between the various levels of society helps to build real bonds of brotherhood and love within the Islamic community and trains those who have, to be generous to those who do not have.

Purpose

The main purpose of *Zakaah al-Fitr* is to provide those who fasted with a means of making up for their errors during the month of fasting. *Zakaah al-Fitr* also provides the poor with a means with which they can celebrate the festival of breaking the fast (*'Eed al-Fitr*) along with the rest of the Muslims. Ibn 'Abbaas reported, *"The Prophet (ﷺ) made **Zakaah al-Fitr** compulsory so that those who fasted may be purified of their idle deeds and shameful talk (committed during Ramadaan) and so that the poor may be fed. Whoever gives it before **Salaah** will have it accepted as **Zakaah,** while he who gives it after **Salaah** has given **Sadaqah**."*[1]

Hence, the goal of *Sadaqah al-Fitr* is the spiritual development of the Believers. By making them give up some of their wealth, the Believers are taught the higher moral characteristics of generosity, compassion (sympathy for the unfortunate), gratitude to God and righteousness. But, since Islaam does not neglect man's material needs, part of the goal of *Zakaah al-Fitr* is the economic well-being of the poorer members of society.

Conditions

Zakaah al-Fitr is only *Waajib* for a particular period of time. If one misses the time period without a good reason, he has sinned and can not make it up. This form of charity becomes obligatory from sunset on the last day of fasting and remains obligatory until the beginning of

---

[1] Collected by Abu Daawood *(Sunan Abu Dawud* (English Trans.), vol. 2, p. 421, no. 1605), and Ibn Maajah and rated *Saheeh* in *Saheeh Sunan Abee Daawood*, vol. 1, p. 303, no. 1420.

Salaah al-'Eed (i.e. shortly after sunrise on the following day). However, it can be paid prior to the above mentioned period, as many of the *Sahaabah* (companions of the Prophet 🕌) used to pay *Sadaqah al-Fitr* a couple of days before the *'Eed*. Naafi' reported that the Prophet's (🕌) companion Ibn 'Umar used to give it to those who would accept it and the people used to give it a day or two before the *'Eed*.[1] *Ibn 'Umar reported that the Prophet (🕌) ordered that it (Zakaah al-Fitr) be given before people go to make the Salaah (al-'Eed).*[2] And Ibn 'Abbaas reported that the Prophet (🕌) said, *"Whoever gives it before the Salaah will have it accepted as Zakaah, while he who gives it after the Salaah (will not, for it will only be considered as) ordinary charity."*[3] Therefore, one who forgets to pay his *Zakaah al-Fitr* on time should do so as soon as possible even though it will not be counted as *Zakaah al-Fitr*.

Rate

The amount of *Zakaah* is the same for everyone regardless of their different income brackets. The minimum amount is one *Saa'* (four handfuls) of food, grain or dried fruit for each member of the family. This calculation is based on Ibn 'Umar's report that the Prophet (🕌) made *Zakaah al-Fitr* compulsory and payable by a *Saa'* of dried dates or a *Saa'* of barley.[4] The *Sahaabee*, Abu Sa'eed al-Khud-

---

[1] Collected by al-Bukhaaree (*Sahih Al-Bukhari* (Arabic-English), vol. 2, p. 339, no. 579), Muslim (*Sahih Muslim* (English Trans.), vol. 2, p. 470, no. 2159) and Abu Daawood (*Sunan Abu Dawud* (English Trans.), vol. 2, p. 421, no. 1606).

[2] Collected by al-Bukhaaree (*Sahih Al-Bukhari* (Arabic-English), vol. 2, p. 342, no. 587) and Abu Daawood (*Sunan Abu Dawud* (English Trans.), vol. 2, p. 421, no. 1606).

[3] Collected by Abu Daawood (*Sunan Abu Dawud* (English Trans.), vol. 2, p. 421, no. 1605) and Ibn Maajah and rated *Saheeh* in *Saheeh Sunan Abee Daawood*, vol. 1, p. 303, no. 1420.

[4] Collected by al-Bukhaaree (*Sahih Al-Bukhari* (Arabic-English), vol. 2, p. 339, no. 580), Muslim (*Sahih Muslim* (English Trans.), vol. 2, p. 468, no. 2149), Abu Daawood (*Sunan Abu Dawud* (English Trans.), vol. 2, p. 422, no. 1607) and Maalik (*Muwatta Imam Malik*, p. 144, no. 691).

ree also said, "In the Prophet's time, we used to give it *(Zakaah al-Fitr)* as a *Saa'* of food, dried dates, barley, raisins or dried cheese."[1]

---

[1] Collected by al-Bukhaaree *(Sahih Al-Bukhari* (Arabic-English), vol. 2, p. 340, no. 582), Muslim *(Sahih Muslim* (English Trans.), vol. 2, p. 469, no. 2155), Abu Daawood *(Sunan Abu Dawud* (English Trans.), vol. 2, p. 423, no. 1612) and Maalik *(Muwatta Imam Malik,* p. 144, no. 692).

QUESTIONS

1. *Zakaah al-Fitr* is the
   (a) name given to charity which must be paid on wealth.
   (b) meal taken at the end of the Ramadaan fast.
   (c) compulsory charity distributed at the end of the Ramadaan fast.
   (d) amount of wealth on which charity is due.
   (e) name given to charity distributed at the end of every year.

2. On whom is *Zakaah al-Fitr* a requirement?

3. Briefly mention three significant points about *Zakaah al-Fitr's* role in society.

4. The main purpose of *Zakaah al-Fitr* in regard to the poor is to
   (a) feed them.
   (b) make them wealthy.
   (c) remove from their hearts feelings of generosity.
   (d) circulate their wealth in the society and prevent hoarding.
   (e) make up for days of fasting which were broken.

5. *Zakaah al-Fitr* becomes obligatory *(Waajib)*
   (a) on the first day of fasting until sunset on the last day of fasting.
   (b) from sunset on the last day of fasting until the beginning of *Salaah al-'Eed.*
   (c) from sunrise on the last day of fasting until sunset on *'Eed* day.
   (d) on the last day of fasting until the end of *Salaah al-'Eed.*
   (e) from sunset on the first day of fasting until the beginning of *Salaah al-'Eed.*

6. If one has not paid *Zakaah al-Fitr* on time he should
   (a) save it until a year has passed on it.
   (b) pay it immediately as ordinary charity.
   (c) fast for ten continuous days.
   (d) keep it as charity.
   (e) give it to his children as a gift.

7. The rate fixed for *Zakaah al-Fiṭr* is
    (a) 2.5%
    (b) 10%
    (c) two *Saa's*
    (d) one *Saa'*
    (e) one handful of silver or gold

8. Mention four differences between *Zakaah* and *Zakaah al-Fiṭr*.

INDEX OF ḤADEETHS

SELECTED BIBLIOGRAPHY

TAWHEED

Ibn 'Abdul Wahhāb, Shaykh Muhammad, *Kitāb Al Tawhīd*, (Kuwait: I.I.F.S.O., 1979), translated by Isma'il al Farūqi.

Philips, Abu ameenah Bilal, *The Fundamentals of Tawheed*, (Riyadh: Tawheed Publications, 1st ed., 1990).

USOOL AT-TAFSEER

Denffer, Ahmad von, *'Ulūm al-Qur'ān*, (U.K.: Islamic Foundation, 1983).

Ibn Taymīyah, Imām, *An Introduction to The Exegesis of The Qur'ān*, (Riyadh: Islamic University of Imam Muhammad Bin Saud, 1989), translated by Muhammad Abdul Haq Ansari.

Maududi, S. Abul A'la, *The Meaning of The Qur'an*, vol. 1, (Lahore: Islamic Publications Ltd., 7th ed., 1984).

Philips, Abu Ameenah Bilal, *Tafseer Soorah al-Hujuraat*, (Riyadh: Tawheed Publications, 2nd ed., 1990).

TAFSEER

Maududi, S. Abul Abul A'la, *The Meaning of The Qur'ān*, vol. xvi, (Lahore: Islamic Publications, 1st ed., 1987).

Qutb, Sayyid, *In The Shade of The Qur'ān*, vol. 30, (London: MWH London Publishers, 1979).

USOOL AL-HADEETH

Abdul Ghaffar, Suhaib Hasan, *Criticism of Hadīth Among Muslims with Reference to Sunan Ibn Mājah*, (U.K.: Ta Ha Publications Ltd., 2nd ed., 1986).

Azami, Muhammad Mustafa, *Studies in Early Hadīth Literature*, (Beirut: al-Maktab al-Islami, 1st ed., 1968).

------------, *Studies in Hadīth Literature,* (Beirut: (U.S.A.: American Trust Publications, 1977).

Robeson, James, *An Introduction to The Science of Tradition by Al-Hākim,* (U.K.: Luzac and Co., Ltd., 1953).

Siddiqi, Muhammad Zubayr, *Hadīth Literature,* (India: Calcutta University, 1961, reissued by Islamic Texts Society, U.K., 1988).

ḤADEETH

Abbasi, Muhammad Yousuf, *Forty Gems: Al-Arba'in by Imam An Nawawi,* (Lahore: Islamic Publications Ltd., 1986).

Abbasi, S.M. Madani, *Riyadh-us-Saleheen,* (Arabic-English), Beirut: Dar Al Arabia, n.d.).

Hasan, Ahmad, *Sunan Abu Dawud,* (English Trans.), Lahore: Sh. Muhammad Ashraf Publishers, 1st ed., 1987.

Khan, Muhammad Muhsin, *Sahīh Al-Bukhāri,* (Arabic-English), Riyadh: Maktabah ar-Riyaad al-Hadeethah, 1981.

Rahimuddin, Muhammad, *Muwatta Imam Malik,* (English Trans.), Lahore: Sh. Muhammad Ashraf Publishers, 1980.

Robeson, James, *Mishkat Al-Masabih,* (English Trans.), Lahore: Sh. Muhammad Ashraf Publishers, 1975.

Siddiq, Abdul Hamid, *Sahih Muslim,* (English Trans.), Lahore: Sh. Muhammad Ashraf Publishers, 1987.

UṢOOL AL-FIQH

Ajijola, A.D., *Introduction of Islamic Law,* (Karachi: International Islamic Publishers, 1981).

Doi, 'Abdur Rahman I., *Shari'ah: The Islamic Law,* (U.K.: Ta Ha Publishers, 1984).

Islahi, Amin Ahsan, *Islamic Law: Concept and Codification,* (Lahore: Islamic Publications Ltd., 1979), translated by S.A. Rauf.

Khudduri, Majid, *al-Shāfi'ī's Risāla,* (U.K.: Islamic Texts Society, 1987).

Masud, Muhammad Khalid, *Islamic Legal Philosophy,* (Islamabad, Pakistan: Islamic Research Institute, 1977).

Muslehuddin, Muhammad, *Philosophy of Islamic Law and The Orientalists,* (Lahore: Islamic Publications Ltd., n.d.).

Philips, Abu Ameenah Bilal, *Evolution of Fiqh: Islamic Law and The Madh-habs,* (Riyadh: Tawheed Publications, 3rd., 1990).

Qadri, Anwar Ahmad, *Islamic Jurisprudence in The Modern World,* (Lahore: Sh. Muhammad Ashraf, 2nd ed., 2nd impression 1981).

FIQH

Qaradawi, Yusuf al-,*The Lawful and The Prohibited in Islam,* (U.S.A.: American Trust Publications, n.d.).

Sabiq, As-Sayyid, *Fiqh us-Sunnah,* vol. III, (U.S.A.: American Trust Publications, 1986).